GIVE US THIS DAY
OUR DAILY RUN . . .

Copyright © 1981 by Christian W. Zauner, Ph.D &
Norma Y. Benson, MPH.
Layout by: Sandy Sharpe
Typeset by: Strehle's Computerized Typesetting,
Ithaca, New York
Printed in the United States of America
by McNaughton Gunn, Ann Arbor, Michigan.

ISBN 0-932392-10-1

GIVE US THIS DAY
OUR DAILY RUN . . .

christian w zauner
norma y benson

Mouvement Publications
109 E. State St.
Ithaca, N.Y. 14850

Box 26 Torquay
Victoria 3228
Australia

18 Kilmorey Park
Chester CH23QS
United Kingdom

CONTENTS

Preface

This book was written with the purpose of presenting an attitude maintained by most habitual exercisers, but rarely expressed. It is more a work of philosophy than a recipe or "how to" directory. We are certain that joggers, runners, swimmers, cyclists, cross-country skiers and all others addicted to physical training will recognize feelings and beliefs they've held but not defined nor verbally expressed, within these covers. Hopefully, our words will join the brotherhood — and sisterhood — with the assurance that spiritual feelings associated with good health and physical well-being are experienced by all who faithfully attend the needs of the body.

Organization of this book varies from the usual, mostly because it is a hybrid of scholarly and entertaining methods. The reader will find some chapters heavily documented. When such is the case, the reference numbers pertain to the Selected References list following the last chapter. In addition, each chapter is closed with a Suggested Reading section. These additional sources are intended to direct the reader with a special interest to expanded treatments of the topic in question.

Not only have we attempted to blend philosophy — theology, almost — with science, but also herein is the ingredient of humor, probably the most underestimated of influences upon human affairs. Perhaps the most important thing one can assimilate through life experiences is that a thing without humor seldom has value. Read and think, yes — but read and smile, too!

Foreword

It is a great pleasure for me to have this opportunity to introduce you to *Give Us This Day Our Daily Run*. The authors have studied and taught for many years the how and why of physical fitness. I can think of no one more qualified to impart to us this knowledge. Chris Zauner and Norma Benson have not only long studied and taught in this area of expertise but have also directly experienced turmoil and triumph in athletics and fitness. Through this book they have provided us with an experience which is educational, inspirational and entertaining.

While teaching and coaching track at the University of Florida, I became aware that it would be beneficial for me to acquire more knowledge regarding physiology of exercise and subsequently enrolled in Dr. Zauner's course. It soon became apparent to me why he was elected "Teacher of the Year" in 1971 at the University of Florida. Difficult material was presented in a most interesting way. That approach has been captured in this book. The reader will find himself racing through technical material with ease and understanding.

Today's modern technology gives us slow-motion film of the great catch at Saturday's football game, computer analysis of an individual gliding through the water, and vast knowledge of sports medicine. Modern Man, therefore, is no longer willing to accept that he should exercise only for the sake of exercise. All of us ask the questions: "Why?" "When?" and "What happens?" *Give Us This Day Our Daily Run* provides the answers to these questions in a way that can be readily understood.

Anyone working in sports or fitness needs to understand biomechanics, physiology of exercise and psychology, as well as the technical aspects of sport skills. Zauner and Benson have knowledge of these aspects, plus years of experience in the classroom and laboratory. Now thousands will have the opportunity to share this information.

We are presently at a peak of interest in physical fitness, and the Olympic Games provide us with more exposure to the concepts of fitness and sport than ever before. Children have opportunities to witness tremendous Olympic performances on television and may be inspired to take part in such activities. Olympic champions, the fittest of the fit, become our heroes. Recent research has shown that the Olympics are ranked by Americans as one of the top events in the world. No doubt many of the 25,000,000 people who are jogging today were inspired to begin when Frank Shorter entered the stadium in Munich to win the 1972 Olympic Marathon. Since that time, there has been a running boom with new sports facilities, running apparel, and sporting goods outlets springing up all over the country. A once nearly unknown event, running has become one of the largest participation activities in existence.

Running has developed into big business. Many companies sponsor runs which provide a means of advertising a product. The people who enter a race, such as the thousands who were in the New York City Marathon, all represent running billboards. In this fashion, support for providing opportunities to achieve physical fitness is forthcoming. People who previously conversed at parties about the local or national football game, now have a conversation piece in their own running performance. Clubs are developing, friendships are made, families are able to train and race together. Where once we heard fishing tales, now we share running tales. There can be no question that we are in the midst of one of the greatest exercise booms ever, and the end is not yet in sight.

It has often been said that the way to success is to fill a need. The free enterprise system in America allows people who have seen a need for a product to develop it, thus gaining success and recognition. Christian Zauner and Norma Benson saw a need and have amply filled it with *Give Us This Day Our Daily Run*. No one who has experienced the challenge, pain, weariness and exhilaration of exercise should omit this book from his reading list.

Jimmy Carnes
President, Athletic Attic and Head Coach, 1980 USA
Olympic Track Team

Acknowledgements

The authors thank the reasearchers cited herein who have provided much of the information included in this volume, and have done so at the expense of years of effort for little, if any, remuneration.

We appreciate also this opportunity to recognize the aid of the countless joggers who have voluntarily provided insights, opinion and participation as research subjects.

Chapter Eleven contains facts and ideas from Roy T. Benson, Chairman, Wellness Department, North Florida Regional Hospital, Gainesville, Florida.

We are grateful to Betty S. Zauner for her excellent cover design.

Last (and no doubt least), the authors acknowledge each other. We always meant to do something like this, and now we have — and it was fun!

C.W.Z.

N.Y.B.

August, 1981

Chapter One

Fitness as a Moral Issue

Morality involves a great deal more than regular church attendance. The philosophers and theologians have written volumes
on the topic. Examination of such literature reveals two basic
facets of morality: first, one must avoid hurting another and, in
addition, every individual has the responsibility to constructively
contribute to society to the fullest extent of his capacity.

The first of these two axioms requires self-examination and
personal evaluation. Learning its full import is often not realized
until later life and following exposure to many people, situations
and cultures. To sacrifice a long-held personal belief in order to
avoid painful conflict with another may well be the epitome of
moral action. This is not entirely synonymous with "turning the
other cheek," however. Morality is not served by acceptance of
indignities or abuse. Weakness is not a virtue. Lions thrive in the
presence of lambs. Protection of one's personal rights and those
of others is an important aspect of moral concern for the individual. Such a function requires mental and physical strength
and endurance. Do *you* have these attributes?

Just as morality is more than religion, so is social success more
than money. Everyone needs to feel as though there is one thing
that he or she does better than do most others, and, furthermore, that this well-done thing makes a significant contribution
to the welfare and progress of mankind. This concept is substan-
tiated by observing that quite wealthy people frequently turn to
charitable endeavor, education or politics for their fulfillment
after discovering that accumulating wealth is no end in itself.

In the final analysis, one's lifetime contribution equals
magnitude of daily productivity times duration of fruitful life.
Success within one's limits of capacity is dependent not only
upon resolve and clarity of thought but upon strength, vigor, efficiency and durability as well. If one cannot be joyfully productive
all day and live out his *full life span,* his potential will not be
realized.

1

Perhaps the greatest moral flaw is failure to meet one's potential. It deprives mankind of all it rightfully expects from each of us. It is an affront to Nature and demeaning to the individual.

From the foregoing, it might appear that the "workaholic" is the modern saint; not true. The workaholic is one who spends much more time than necessary to get the job done. He is driven to produce by an innate sense of morality but lacks efficiency to accomplish it. By ignoring physical needs and thereby abusing his body he renders himself continuously less capable of meeting his own demands. Daily productivity is diminished and life span shortened. Potential is never realized. The moral flaw is evident.

The human body is made for activity. Scientific research clearly shows it to thrive on physical exercise (35,43,53,79,86,107,109). Yet pursuits of sophisticated, educated and intelligent men are rarely physical in nature. Great contributions to modern society are most frequently made by the mind, the exceptions being those provided by the truly gifted athlete or dancer. Logic would seem to dictate that most of us need to therefore cultivate the mind and neglect the body. But stamina, strength and vigor are not generated by the thought processes. Regularly taken exercise is required to create and maintain these components of fitness. Physical activity becomes a requisite to moral action.

Athough it is an old chestnut indeed, consider the Roman Empire. What preceded the fall of that great civilization, or the fall of many others, for that matter? One is tempted to parrot ". . . moral decadence. . . ." But that is a half-answer, at best. List the symptoms of moral decadence and the outcome is a description of spectatoritis. Is there a real difference between observing the Lions versus the Christians as opposed to the Lions versus the Rams? Furthermore, are slavery, gluttony and deteriorating physical status (lack of moral action) aspects only of ancient civilizations?

In fallen civilizations, contributions to society became entirely secondary to personal aggrandizement. The "hooray for me and to hell with you" attitude dominated, and that attitude permeates modern social structure as well.

How could the thirteen American Colonies defeat the forces of the British Empire? Why were the crude Teutonic hordes able to devastate Rome? What enabled the impoverished Russian working class to overthrow the powerful czar? What magic did the Viet Cong employ to ward off advances of immense American military might? Was it strong moral fiber? Or great physical stamina and strength? Or are these really one?

We need to strive for the good life, but we must not fall victim to it. Indeed, it is critical to genuine progress that we create a better environment for man; but also recognize the stimulating effect of deprivation and physical stress. Observe the needs to contribute and to spare others pain, but understand as well that one has a responsibility to oneself, for moral action cannot follow physical neglect.

Every religion says it. In one form or another it is found in the Old and New Testaments, The Talmud, The Koran, the writings of Buddha, and of Confucius — ". . . defile not the Temple of God. . . ." And where does God live? He lives within each of us. *Your* body is His temple. He who ignores this temple will surely be even more severely judged than those who lie, cheat and steal.

SUGGESTED READING

Abdalati, H., *Islam in Focus.* Indianapolis: American Trust Publication, 1975. Pp. xv + 211.

Burtt, E. A., (ed.), *The Teachings of the Compassionate Buddha.* New York: The New American Library of World Literature, 1955. Pp. 247.

Downs, R. B., *Books That Changed the World.* New York: The New American Library, 1956. Pp. 200.

Maududi, A. A., *Towards Understanding Islam.* Beirut: The Holy Koran Publishing House, 1980. Pp xi + 179.

More, T., *Utopia.* New York: Appleton-Century-Crofts, Inc., 1949. Pp. xii + 84.

Chapter Two

Pity the Poor Mesomorph

Sheldon defines the mesomorph as one whose primary structural component is muscle tissue (121). Of all people, why pity *him?* After all, he was the idolized and envied athlete in his youth. Just think of all the lovely girls who smiled upon him! Didn't his apparent robust health and rosy appearance make favorable impressions at job interviews, thereby leading to current success? Strong, healthy, attractive and successful — what need pity?

Perhaps the answer lies in the past. With just a little imagination one can picture the mesomorph as a caveman among his more boney (ectomorphic) and fatty (endomorphic) peers. Because of greater strength, speed and endurance, in this almost solely physical pre-historic world the mesomorph surely dominated. He was most likely to succeed in the hunt and thereby provide sustenance for himself and for others. One has difficulty seeing the endomorph chasing down a zebra or the ectomorph out-wrestling a wild boar. A leadership role was assuredly assigned to the mesomorph. One can imagine him advising, "Do what I say or this stone axe will make an impression on you." Who should argue? The Stone Age woman, recognizing her weakness during pregnancy in this hostile environment, undoubtedly preferred the mesomorph as a mate. He was a good provider and an excellent protector. In battle the mesomorph was best able to protect himself and most efficiently equipped to inflict his will upon others. Successful, valued in his society, well-fed, popular with the ladies — it surely appears that the mesomorphic need for pity does not originate in the past! But don't close out the possibility.

Jousting has been known to be wearing on a man. Could it be that the mesomorph's pitiable condition is associated with medieval times? When jousting, the knight wore a suit of armor that may have outweighed him. The lance was three times his height, held with tip high and no counter-balance. Strength of

4

leg must have been important to maintain position astride the charger, especially when approaching the opponent at full gallop. Also, what kind of strength and agility were required to rescue damsels in distress, not to mention that needed to combat a dragon? Knights were more than likely mesomorphs, still admired and still valued. Still no answer.

Conditions were considerably less primitive, albeit rather stressful, in the days of the early American West. Guns replaced stone axes and lances. Surely not much muscle is required for the traditional trigger squeeze. Let us examine the cowboy: sufficiently durable to ride horseback twelve hours daily; adequate strength to hold down a frightened calf for branding; agility to spin about, drop to the ground, draw and fire at the enemy in a single motion. These are not traits of the ectomorph nor of the endomorph. The mesomorph wins in this environment, too!

The mesomorph was uniquely well endowed as farmer, herder and industrial worker as well. Until about a century ago, as a matter of fact, the mesomorph had a distinct advantage over others in regard to coping with life. Only in recent years has the environment become so refined that superior strength and endurance have been less than necessary for survival. Furthermore, laws of modern civilization properly protect the weak. Were Davy Crockett alive today, he'd be in jail — and the bear he "kilt" would be in a zoo.

The problems of the mesomorph most certainly are of recent origin. He continues to place himself in challenging positions. American presidents (both Roosevelts, Eisenhower, Ford, Kennedy, Reagan) are usually mesomorphic, as are many lower echelon national leaders (Senator Robert Mathias, Supreme Court Justice "Whizzer" White, Senator Edward Kennedy). Great leaders of business and industry often share this characteristic, as do members of the professions. Mesomorphs still frequently are wealthy, powerful and admired, only natural since they have, in effect, been selecting out parameters of success for themselves for generations. So why the need for sympathy?

The modern challenges are not of a physical nature. They force a sedentary lifestyle upon those who pursue them. The mesomorph has the personal drive, ambition and dedication to meet such challenges, but his body is unsuited for it. From the point of viw of his physical welfare, the mesomorph would be far better off chasing zebras or wrestling wart hogs.

Proof of the mesomorphic dilemma is at hand. A population

of hospital patients confined due to heart disease has been described as mesomorphic (61). Polycythemia, a disease of pathologically increased numbers of red blood cells leading to increased blood viscosity and elevated blood pressure, is almost solely confined to the mesomorph (116). Mesomorphs are more inclined to suffer hypertension (61) and to experience ulcers of the digestive tract. Acquired obesity is more often a problem for the mesomorph than for other body types (32). Perhaps needless to say, the mesomorph has a higher incidence of heart and artery disease than do his ectomorphic and endomorphic brothers (44).

Pity is a charitable expression but it is ineffective. What is to be done about the mesomorph? One is tempted to suggest that since he has done so well, let him now pay his dues. After all, he has thrived all this time on the law of survival of the fittest. Although it may be ironic, it now appears that the mesomorph is least fit to survive in present conditions. Let nature take its course. Let him fade out.

There are two problems with the survival of the fittest solution. First of all, the mesomorph makes too vast a social contribution to allow him to phase out. And furthermore, when we talk about sacrificing the mesomorph to nature — we are more than likely talking about ourselves! Mesomorphic success in earlier environments has (naturally) resulted in a predominantly mesomorphic human population. Allowing the mesomorph to become extinct by ignoring his problems is akin to genocide.

There is a solution, although, as with most efforts to conserve important natural resources, it is a partial one at best. In a step-by-step progression, one needs to:

1. Inform the mesomorph (you?) of his predisposing factors,
2. examine for existing health problems,
3. add mild but progressive supervised rhythmic physical activity to his lifestyle,
4. educate regarding proper habits of diet and rest, and
5. reevaluate the now active and dieting mesomorph's health status frequently.

The answer is simple and easy to apply. All knowledge and resources required for implementing the solution are available. Take steps to conserve the endangered mesomorph now! Remember, "The life you save may be your own!"

But, if you're too tired or too busy or if the thought of perspiring seems beneath you, then just forget it. We are overpopulated anyway. Your early demise will allow more room for those of us who have learned to adapt to the changing environment.

SUGGESTED READING

Mathews, D. K. and Fox, E. L., *The Physiological Basis of Physical Education and Athletics*. Phila.: W. B. Saunders, Co., 1976. Pp. xvi + 577.

Sheldon, W. H., *The Varieties of Human Physique*. New York: Harper and Brothers Publishers, 1940. Pp. xiv + 347.

Chapter Three

The Evolution Lag

Man has a magnificent brain. In particular, the cerebral cortex is extremely well-developed, unrivaled in all the animal kingdom, save perhaps by that of the dolphin. The complexity of Man's cerebral cortex is enormous, such that only a very few are qualified to discuss it. However, it is reported to house uniquely human characteristics — intelligence, memory, ability to manipulate abstractions and to differentiate right from wrong. Furthermore, Man is the only animal who can readily oppose his thumb to each of his other upper extremity digits. He can, therefore, not only grasp tools (stones, clubs, axes, hammers, hoes, electric drills) but also delicately manipulate them (grinding implements, screw drivers, micrometers, the abacus, calculators, computors). With these two attributes (the brain and the thumb) we have been able to greatly facilitate our social evolution. We have structured social systems, philosophies, religions, industries, money systems and political theories. Man can now enjoy logically assigned periods of work, rest and play, being no longer tied entirely to the whims of weather, the luck of the hunt or to the habits of other animals. Great labor saving devices relieve him of drudgery and clever inventions provide entertainment and vicarious experiences. In western civilization in particular, comfort and ease are rampant.

A vestigial organ is one which physically remains but which is without original function. Man has but two readily identifiable vestigial organs — the small toe and the veriform appendix. Only a very unusual person could remember the last time he used his little toe, discounting stubbing it painfully on a projecting chair leg. If one is conscious of it at all, it is when it gets in the way. Yet, the small toe perhaps, was a valuable appendage to one of our tree-dwelling, limb-grasping predecessors, just as was the third intestine, now represented by the appendix. Cooking is really a form of pre-digestion. Before our tree-dwelling relative discovered cooking (some say it was either an early Frenchman or a Peking Man) probably by accidentally dropping the duck in the campfire, he required an extra length of intestine to complete digestion of raw food.

The vestigial organs are disappearing. When something is not used, it atrophies. One can see that the small toe is indeed small, and the appendix is about the size of the little finger. Once in awhile on the beach, one can observe a four-toed individual who, incidentally, should not feel deprived since his difference merely represents further evolutionary progress than most have made. Although there is absolutely no evidence to support the concept, one might hypothesize that many who have never had an attack of appendicitis have been spared this agony because they haven't got an appendix.

And now we approach a sensitive issue. Man may have a third vestigal organ, i.e., hair, especially that on the head, particularly vestigal in the male of the species. Head hair at one time protected against blows from the irate neighbor's club. That the uncombed and matted hair could serve in this capacity is clearly demonstrated by pre-adolescent boys of today. Although hair may be "in," it is definitely on the way out.

Two, and possibly three, vestigial organs are all we have to show for centuries of existence. This should tell us something. It should inform us that we evolve much more slowly physiologically than we do socially. Our social evolution has outstripped by far our physiological adaptation. In fact, our fantastic brain and magnificent thumb have about done us in, for they have allowed enormous advancement relative to the nature of our environment, while the physical being has remained appropriate for far more primitive conditions.

It is possible today to live without much physical effort. Acquiring food is no longer an infrequent proposition requiring skill, luck, knowledge and effort. It is just a matter of opening the refrigerator or, at most, riding in the car to the super market. Yet, the body continues to store calories in the form of fat just as though it were likely that the next meal would be associated with the next kill, which might be days away.

When our early ancestors experienced stress it was no doubt usually associated with a kill-or-be-killed situation. And, of course, what one killed, one ate. It was functionally appropriate in those days for stress to elicit secretion of digestive enzymes as well as hormones like adrenaline that prepare one for great physical effort. Modern man, lagging drastically in regard to his personal evolution, continues to respond to stress as did his early ancestors. However, most stress today is associated neither with impending physical effort nor with eating. When the boss describes the employee's inadequacies, the enzymes and hormones flow. Corrosive digestive substances, in the absence of food in the tract, will irritate delicate membranes lining the stomach and small intestine. The result may well be the typical executive duodenal ulcer. In addition, adrenaline prepares one to either punch the boss or flee from him. Do either, and dismissal and probably incarceration will result. There can be no physical outlet, yet the heart rate is up, the cardiac output is increased, the airways are dilated, some of the blood vessels are constricted and the blood pressure is elevated. That is a lot like hypertension.

Have you heard of the pathological eater? In times of personal stress, he eats. Gross obesity is the outcome. He merely mirrors the ages-old reflex — stress means food. But today, one doesn't hunt. One opens another package of potato chips and pops a can of soda. While the pathologic eating routine is comforting, easy and probably prevents stomach ulcers, it precipitates a deadly vicious cycle; i.e., "The more I eat the fatter I get which is stressful to me so I eat still more and get still fatter."

Can we wait for Man's physiological evolution to catch up with his social progress? Not likely, since social advancements continue to accumulate. We are on a treadmill that ever moves too fast and we continue to fall behind. Furthermore, even if waiting were possible, history has shown physical softness to come before moral, mental and social deterioration. It looks as though we are restricted to doing things to pamper our retarded bodies.

We could, instead, recognize that labor-savers and mental, rather than physical endeavors, are energy conservers, and that therefore, our habit of "three square meals a day" may no longer be appropriate. We could, when under stress, turn away from the artificial kill (bag of chips) and toward the artificial hunt (exercise).

The scientific literature has long supported the notion that adaptation to exercise stress transfers to stress from other sources (119). If one is successfully adapted to jogging, one can safely worry more! Responses to derogatory comments from people important in one's life can better be withstood if the body has learned to deal with adaptations to exercise stress. When the adrenaline flows, those good exercise habits will provide an eventual outlet.

Nature can be a best friend or the worst enemy. Her impetuousness that so intrigues us can be a deceit that threatens existence. Blue-water sailors may be best able to attest to this. A placid lovely day at sea is likely to be followed by a devastating, death-dealing storm. Be careful now, that mistress Nature doesn't unexpectedly turn upon us as we sip beer comfortably in our easy chairs, watching the tube. Our great natural assets — brain and thumb — have created all this ease. It is a product of Man's superiority — his natural execllence in an environment he has significantly altered. But be not deceived. This world still belongs to the fleet of foot and strong of limb!

SUGGESTED READING

Freeman, W. H., *Physical Education in a Changing Society*. Boston: Houghton Mifflin Co., 1977. Pp. xiv + 323.

Larsen, O. A. and Malmborg, R. O. (eds.), *Coronary Heart Disease and Physical Fitness*. Copenhagen: Munksgaard, 1971. Pp. 277.

Raab, W. (ed.), *Prevention of Ischemic Heart Disease: Principles and Practice*. Springfield, Ill.: Charles C. Thomas, Publisher, 1966. Pp. xxxiii + 466.

Toffler, A., *Future Shock*. New York: Bantam Books, 1970. Pp. xiv + 561.

Chapter Four

Melon Belly as Status Symbol

If you had a Great Aunt Mamie as I had, somewhere in her house was an oil portrait or early tin-type of Great Grandfather Thadeus. His most memorable feature was an immense expanse of vest-covered and watch chain-draped abdomen. Here was a man of means and importance.

In the United States Navy there is a traditional service honoring advancement from first-class to chief petty officer in which the new chief is fed a meal of unlimited proportions from a wooden trough. This ceremony suggests that the advancement results in the good and easy life, best symbolized by food in plenty. And, in retrospect, I cannot recall a chief without a belly.

When traveling by car, particularly in the South, have you noticed the road-working crews? Even during a break (There seems to be a bunch of those!) one can easily separate the supervisor from the laborers simply on the basis of magnitude of abdominal girth. The superiors clearly identify that they need no longer labor to acquire a superbly adequate diet.

And then there is the Gerber baby — cute, chubby, obviously well fed and healthy! Related to that might be my mother's attitude in my childhood which also coincided with the Great Depression. Dad was the only man on the block with a job. "Eat," Mother would say, "you're so skinny the neighbors will think your father is out of work." Had I had a stomach, it would have been our Cadillac in the driveway!

During the Korean Conflict a number of young American soldiers killed in action were examined by autopsy and found to have suffered fairly extensive atherosclerosis — fat deposits in the arteries — a common outcome of overeating. No such pathology was reported from autopsies of South Korean soldiers. Here were young "fit" Americans showing clear evidence of a disease associated with later life. Could it be that this result of overeating and under-exercising begins in infancy or childhood but delays demonstration of symptoms until middle-age?

One of my sisters is twelve years younger than I. I clearly recall that her formula in infancy was comprised almost entirely of condensed milk and corn syrup, a concoction richer in fat, carbohydrates and calories than human mother's milk. Futhermore, her strict feeding schedule required that she be awakened and fed if discovered to be sleeping through a mealtime. My own children were raised in a similar fashion upon advice from the pediatrician, who conceived of skim milk as something to be thrown out after making butter.

The history of man is such that our consideration of food as goodness is quite understandable. The successful caveman was bound to show nutritional evidence of his skill as a hunter, as was the quality farmer and herder. There is some documentation that in ancient times, periods of famine were followed by periods of plenty — that bad times were associated with lack of food and good times with dietary opulence. Even mythology and other literature forms demonstrate heroes and nice guys who are obviously well nourished (Zeus, Santa Claus) while those who are less than heroic or villainous are depicted as lean and spare (Ichabod Crane, Count Dracula). Fat people are stereotyped as jolly and generous; thin individuals as mean and miserly. Today, important people are commonly known as "big men" — big on campus, big in athletics, big in business. Little boys ache to grow up to weigh at least two hundred pounds — just like Dad.

Yes, some people do indeed think of the damndest things. But really, doesn't it appear as though Western Civilization is at least inclined toward placing value on the melon belly? Weird — but the evidence is there! To contemplate the condition is amusing, but serious consideration of consequences of such valuation is frightening.

Consider that the United States has an extremely high incidence of heart and artery disease (8), that faulty metabolism of ingested fat is clearly related to such problems (10,11,18,57) and futhermore, that diet rich in fat is also linked to incidence of coronary artery disease (19,50). Research has shown that obesity is a predisposing factor for heart disease (5,55). As we grow older, blood fat levels increase (3,22) and our abilities to metabolize ingested fats depreciate (141). This latter failing may well be inhibited by introducing habitual physical activity to the lifestyle (138), although once incurred, abnormal fat metabolism is not likely to be changed by training (139). In other words, being a big man probably leads to a proliferation of health problems and, quite likely, an early demise. In addition to a status symbol, the melon belly is a danger signal.

Fortunately, today there seems to be a trend away from obvious over-nourishment as a status symbol. The slim look is in, for men as well as women. More and more people are becoming figure, diet and exercise conscious. Patronizing a "big man" shop has lost some of its prestige. Perhaps coincidentally, the rate of increase of heart and artery disease in the United States has, at last, leveled off.

But there are other things we can and must do. Middle-aged and older people have to realize that age beyond thirty years usually brings a reduction in resting metabolism and that, therefore, we need less food at those times of our lives. Young mothers must be convinced that fat children are *not* healthy children. A study has shown, for instance, that far too many of our suburban, middle-class youngsters are pathologically obese (27). The *lean* child is the healthy child, learning early to avoid poor habits of diet and exercise that initiate disease processes which show their symptoms later in life. All of us need to understand that the so-called modern afflictions (heart disease, stroke, hypertension, obesity, obstructive lung diseases) are not death-dealing ailments that arrive full-blown in late adulthood but rather insidious, growing entities that begin to damage in childhood — perhaps in infancy. It may well be true that one begins to die on the day of his birth.

Finally, we need help from the medical profession. Somehow, doctors must be made able to realize that daily exercise is as necessary to continued good health as is an appropriate daily sleep period. Their training should include subject material that will enable them to prescribe exercise even as they prescribe drugs, and to furthermore produce in the young doctor the certainty that normal exercise is often the therapy of choice, as opposed to convenient use of foreign chemical substances. The gynocologist should know that pregnancy is a normal event and that physical activity has been observed to facilitate the child bearing process (40). The pediatrician must see the chubby child as not the epitome of good health but instead an individual showing early signs of a pathological condition. And just as important, future medical education has to include extensive study of diet in order that lay people have the opportunity to turn to someone other than the prepared food producers for advice in this area.

Hey! a motto for TODAY — We're sellin' the melon, 'cause thin is in!

SUGGESTED READING

Kannel, W. B., The disease of living. *Nutrition Today*, 6:2-11, 1971.

Leveille, G. A. and Rosmos, D. R., Meal eating and obesity. *Nutrition Today*, 9:4-9, 1974.

Montoye, H. J., *Physical Activity and Health: An Epidemiological Study of an Entire Community*. Englewood Cliffs, N.J.: Prentice-Hall, Inc., 1975. Pp. xv + 205.

Chapter Five

Physiology of a Run

In its broadest definition, physiology is function. Human physiology, then, is how one's body works. Some aspects of human physiology are indeed complex, but much, with simple explanation, can be readily understood. The purpose of this chapter is to enable the reader to understand the functional things that occur to and within the body during a rather long run. It is, in fact, a lesson in the physiology of exercise, an honorable discipline with a long and interesting history.

As a rule, one anticipates running before he begins to do so. When such is the case, a number of changes, preparatory in nature, occur. That these alterations are in fact happening is often signaled by the familiar "butterflies in the stomach" syndrome. Although it may appear otherwise, this adaptation is favorable to later performance. It should never be interpreted as weakness or a lack of readiness.

Awareness of an approaching physical task activates our two major energy spending systems — the sympathetic nervous system and the adrenal medulla. The sympathetic nerves are those that spring from the spinal cord to service many of the bodily organs. When stimulated, these nerves aid the liver to increase blood sugar concentration, stimulate sweat glands, speed up the heart and encourage increased breathing rate and depth.

The adrenal glands are located close to the kidneys. The medulla makes up the inner core of each of the members of this pair of glands. The adrenal medulla secretes the hormones eperephrine and norepinephrine which enlarge airways in the lungs, facilitate cardiac activity and assist in mobilizing energy yielding substances from fat stored on the body.

In view of these potentials for alterations in the body's internal environment which are precipitated by anticipation of exercise, it seems evident that, in a sense, the body becomes prepared for the upcoming challenge. It is more or less analogous to stepping lightly on the gas a bit prior to engaging the clutch. In the case of the human body, anticipating exercise leads to moderate increases in rate and depth of breathing, mobilization of energy yielding stores, and in heart rate. This elevation in heart rate is accompanied by a larger amount of blood pumped by the heart at each beat. Since cardiac output (the amount of blood pumped by the heart in a minute) is the product of heart rate times how much blood departs the heart in a single beat, it is evident that anticipation of exercise also results in increased cardiac output.

All blood that passes through the lungs is pumped by the right side of the heart. Blood is the only bodily agent that can absorb oxygen, and it does so only in the lungs. Therefore, when cardiac output is accelerated, blood flow through the lungs is increased leading to an increase in amount of oxygen absorbed by the body per unit of time. The extra oxygen taken up at the lungs when anticipating exercise is subsequently delivered by the blood to cells all over the body, most particularly to the muscle cells. Increased oxygen delivery to cells stimulates metabolism in those cells; they produce more energy.

Your body is about 20 percent efficient. That is to say, only about 20 percent of energy released in cells is used to accomplish measurable work. The remaining 80 percent is given off as heat. The body temperature is a reflection of this phenomenon. Of course the heat produced needs to be eliminated in some way since accumulated quantities would damage cells. For this reason, increases in energy production by cells is accompanied by intensification of effort by the body to dissipate heat. One begins to perspire and to direct blood to the skin when body temperature rises. An outcome of anticipation of exercise is appearance of light perspiration on the skin.

In short, the approaching exercise is prepared for nicely in the form of increased oxygen uptake, stimulated circulation, greater cooling of the body and mobilization of energy stores. And the butterflies? That phenomenon is due, for the most part to constriction of large veins in the central circulation which leads to a shunt, or redirection, of blood away from tissues unimportant in exercise to the peripheral vessels in the muscles and skin. A short walk and a little stretching, and you and your butterflies are ready for the start!

As you begin your run, your body continues to adapt. First, the veins lying between muscles in the legs are subjected to pressure with each muscular contraction. Since valves in the veins permit blood to move only toward the heart, this milking action hastens blood through the veins to the heart. The activity

17

of this "muscle pump" both evacuates the blood from the legs, permitting inflow of freshly oxygenated blood, and also further stimulates cardiac output, since whatever the heart accepts it must subsequently put out. A hastened return of blood to the heart elevates both heart rate and stroke volume, the amount of blood expelled by the heart at each beat. As mentioned previously, since cardiac output per minute equals heart rate per minute times stroke volume, it is evident that the "muscle pump" facilitates cardiac output.

Contracting muscle generates heat and produces acid waste. The presence of heat and acid dilates capillaries and permits increased perfusion of the tissue with blood. It has been estimated that blood flow through a working muscle is increased over rest by a factor of fifty. Oxygen utilization in muscle is partially dependent, of course, upon delivery rate of oxygen. Blood represents the oxygen delivery system. The fifty-fold increase in blood flow in contracting muscle is responsible in part for an estimated one hundred-fold increase in oxygen uptake by muscle during heavy exercise. Oxygen use by muscle is further stimulated because hemoglobin in blood surrenders constantly increasing quantities of oxygen in the face of decreasing presence of that gas. In other words, exercise, by using oxygen, produces an "oxygen sink" into which greater quantities of the gas can flow.

In addition to heat and acid waste, muscle produces carbon dioxide. But carbon dioxide is more than a simple waste product. It has a powerful influence on respiration and on cardiac activity. The carbon dioxide produced in muscle is picked up and carried by the blood to the lungs, where it is excreted. However, as exercise continues there is a significant build-up of carbon dioxide in the blood. As the amount of this gas rises in the blood, it causes a reflex increase in respiratory rate and depth. Respiration is similarly stimulated by a neural reflex initiated through receptors located in muscles and joints. Elevated blood carbon dioxide also increases heart rate. Countering this response is the effect of increasing blood pressure, which accompanies exercise, and leads to a depression of heart rate. Although these antagonistic actions may seem paradoxical, the end effect is to accelerate heart rate sufficiently to allow greater cardiac output while permitting adequate time between beats for filling of the heart chambers.

Heat produced in the muscle during exercise increases in quantity and must be dissipated. The body attends to this by opening still more capillaries just under the skin, permitting blood to carry heat to the surface where it can be transferred to the environment by convection. More perspiration appears on the skin and evaporates, thus aiding in heat dissipation.

As can be seen, demand for blood is at the muscle and at the skin during exercise. To achieve this, central circulation, especially that to the viscera, is cut back. The visceral organs are deprived of adequate blood flow and largely shut down their function. For instance, during heavy exercise digestion and absorption very nearly stop, as does urine formation.

So, as you jog along, heart rate, cardiac stroke volume and cardiac output all increase, serving to permit greater oxygen uptake at the lungs, more rapid oxygen delivery to the muscles and greater perfusion of the working muscle. Furthermore, respiratory rate and depth increase and, hand in hand with greater blood flow through the lungs, allow for more rapid diffusion of oxygen across the lung membrane into blood. Heat and acid produced by exercising muscle dilate vessels in the muscle and aid in the unloading of oxygen at that site. Blood is shunted from places not needed to muscle and skin. All systems act to allow for the immense demands placed upon the body in terms of energy release, waste removal and heat dissipation.

The jogger generally achieves a steady state during his activity at which time he is capable of bringing in very nearly enough oxygen for the task at hand, and to eliminate waste and heat almost as rapidly as they are created. For most joggers, male or female, the steady state is accompanied by a heart rate of about 140-150 beats per minute and a body temperature approximately one degree Centigrade greater than that at rest. Whole body oxygen uptake increases by a factor of nearly ten and cardiac output is likely to approximately double or perhaps triple during steady state exercise.

As long as one remains at the pace that precipitates the steady state, things go along rather smoothly. But what happens when the pace is increased? In an effort to continue to bring in adequate oxygen and eliminate larger quantities of waste and heat, there are further increments in heart rate, cardiac output, respiratory rate and depth, whole body oxygen uptake and skin perfusion. However, extremely heavy exercise cannot be supported by these so-called aerobic adaptations. To an ever greater extent, energy must be released by anaerobic mechanisms, those that can occur without involvement of oxygen. This is an inefficient mechanism and results in accumulation of waste products. The internal environment begins to change. Body temperature soars and high levels of carbon dioxide cause the acidity of the blood to rise. When making a maximal physical effort, the heart rate might exeed 200 beats per minute and the cardiac output sometimes approaches nearly a six-fold increase over that at rest. The central body temperature may reach three degrees Centigrade above resting and oxygen uptake may increase by as much as fifteen times its resting value. It is rare for the breathing rate to exceed 40 breaths per minute, even at maximal work.

Usually joggers and those who train by slow swimming are operating at about 60-70 percent of their maximal aerobic (oxygen supported) power. For most individuals this is representative of an altogether safe yet effective level of effort. How does one know that he is functioning at this appropriate level? Surely he cannot constantly monitor cardiac output or oxygen uptake. Fortunately, when one is functioning at about 70% of maximal aerobic power, his heart rate will be about 70% of its maximal as well.

There are a number of ways to measure or estimate maximal heart rate. However, these methods are not available to all. Therefore, considering that average maximal heart rate approaches 200 beats per minute, as a rule of thumb a safe and effective training heart rate would be about 140 bpm. A caution — maximal heart rate depreciates with age. If you are planning to use our rule of thumb, reduce the suggested 140 by five beats each decade beyond 50 years of age. That is to say, if you are between 50 and 60 years old, train at 135 bpm, or at 130 bpm if you are between 60 and 70. Better still, first consult your physician and then find someone who will measure you and extract an age and fitness-compensated training heart rate.

Now, on your next run, listen to your body and see if it isn't ticking along about as described. Especially, check your pulse periodically. Derive the minute rate from a six or 10 second count. Longer counts are falsely low since heart rate slows rapidly as soon as exercise ceases. If your minute rate exceeds 140 (or 150 if you are really well-trained) you are probably over-doing. If it is less than 130 or 140 you may be wasting some time. As a final check, count your heart rate 10 minutes following your jog. If it is more than 100 bpm, you may have over-exerted.

A few guidelines can make an activity more enjoyable. But the real joy of jogging lies not in estimating aerobic capacity, but rather in the freedom and separation that are intrinsic to the sport. Don't go overboard on pulse counts. With very little practice you can easily relate pace, feelings or breathing rate to how hard you are working as reflected by heart rate. Run smoothly, smile, talk. If you can do those things the pump is probably working well!

SUGGESTED READING

Costill, D. L., *What Research Tells the Coach about Distance Running.* Washington, D.C.: American Association for Health, Physical Education and Recreation, 1968. Pp. vi + 49.

Fox, E. L., *Sports Physiology.* Philadelphia: W. B. Saunders, Co., 1979. Pp. xii + 383.

Guyton, A. C., *Textbook of Medical Physiology* (6th ed.). Phila.: W. B. Saunders Co., 1980, Pp. xxxvi + 1194.

Lamb, D. R., *Physiology of Exercise.* New York: Macmillan Publishing Co., Inc., 1978. Pp. xx + 438.

Morehouse, L. E. and Miller, A. T., Jr., *Physiology of Exercise* (7th ed.). St. Louis: The C. V. Mosby Co., 1976. Pp. xii + 364.

Chapter Six

Outcomes of Habitual Physical Activity

Training is task specific. That is to say, the body adapts in such a manner as to more efficiently perform whatever is asked of it. That's why muscles, for instance, get stronger when required to overcome progressively heavier resistances, or, for that matter, why they become weaker when asked to do little or nothing. Therefore, training becomes rather a shopping expedition. How one trains is dictated by the outcomes desired. If muscular strength and power are sought, it's in to the weight room. A need to improve heart and lung function, on the other hand, is best met on the track or in the pool. It is necessary then, to identify objectives prior to launching the training program.

For the sake of this essay, let us restrict our examination to that of an initially sedentary male of about 40 years of age who has elected to train by means of jogging on weekdays and by utilizing light weights three times a week for upper body exercises. What training outcomes can be expected?

If our subject knows to begin his jogging program by walking, and his weight training with very light weights and few repetitions, and if he precedes each training session with a period of stretching, the traditional early training soreness and stiffness can be largely avoided. Furthermore, such practices allow gradual adaptation of muscle and connective tissue so that few, if any, days will be lost due to minor injuries to those tissues. A slow start with gradual increments is essential. The bone-throbbing pain many associate with early experiences at "getting in shape" is absolutely unnecessary. Training progressions ought to be achieved naturally — done when they feel right, rather than according to some arbitrary schedule. And, temporary regressions are a normal aspect of long-term training. If today seems to demand a slower, shorter or lighter workout, oblige — tomorrow is another day.

After just a few days our now-active 40-year-old friend will notice a feeling of well-being, renewed energies and a tendency to sleep better. Those outcomes are encouraging, beneficial and useful — but not physiological. Early "feelings" are rarely measurable in the laboratory. The participant experiences them because he heard he was supposed to, and because of his pleasure at finally doing something difficult — something physically challenging — and doing it for himself. These first-week sensations are purely psychological. Psychological also are the strength increases, as evidenced by ability to work with heavier weights, often noted after only several days of training. These increments are reflective of the psychological aspect of the so-called "Disinhibition Theory of Muscular Strength Development" which hypothesizes that even minimal experience with weight training will reduce mental barriers to dealing with heavy work. The physiological half of the Disinhibition Theory, activated following a month or more of training, will be discussed later in this chapter. Even though these early "changes" are psychological rather than physiological, their importance as motivating factors must not be minimized. As with any endeavor, when successes and satisfying feedback exceed failures and painful experiences, continuation is ensured.

Genuine physiological changes in the muscle can generally be expected to appear in our 40-year-old trainee after a month or six weeks of working with weights. At that time, a measurable increase in the size of each trained muscle fiber is evident, a phenomenon properly known as muscle fiber hypertrophy (51). Hypertrophy underlies strength increases which, of course, occur at the same time (96). Fiber hypertrophy and increased muscular strength are most likely to happen when weight training includes regular increments in weight moved, and are not grossly affected by programs in which training increments are in the form of elevations in repetitions with weight held constant.

Improvement in muscular endurance (the number of times a muscle can overcome a given submaximal resistance) usually comes somewhat after strength increments. Muscular endurance is, in the main, a function of oxygen delivery to the contracting tissue (45). It coincides with measurable increases in extensiveness of capillary beds in muscle (145), a training outcome that allows for better blood flow through the trained muscle. Superior muscular endurance is achieved through application of over-load in the form of increased repetitions of a movement against a resistance that remains relatively constant during a training period. Most who train for purposes of physical maintenance usually strive for maximal endurance outcomes and minimal strength development, and achieve this by working toward many repetitions (50 or more) of a given exercise with quite light weights (five to 20 pounds, dependent upon muscle groups used).

Measurable physiological outcomes of the jogging regimen are likely to appear in our subject following about six weeks of involvement. Perhaps the earliest observable improvement is a reduction in heart rate at rest (90) and at submaximal exercise (128). We have observed decreases of up to ten beats per minute after six weeks of training in both resting heart rate and that noted while treadmill walking at 3.5 mph and at a 5% grade. Incidentally, since so many factors influence heart rate, it is best to count it upon awakening following a full night's sleep, and prior to arising. A treadmill is not necessary for measuring heart rate at submaximal work. A convenient way to do this is to simply note the heart rate upon completing a walk of standard distance and speed, and under similar conditions of environmental temperature and humidity. Exercise heart rate should be counted for no more than ten seconds and corrected to a minute count, since it depreciates rapidly upon cessation of physical activity. The latter observation leads to the next point. Training by continuous rhythmic activity, such as by jogging, early leads to more rapid recovery of heart rate toward the resting value after a given exercise task (101). Although laboratory techniques do exist for estimation of this parameter, our jogger can check this for himself by counting heart rate for ten seconds, one, three and five minutes following a standard walk or jog. In the same vein, generally over-exertion is indicated when heart rate fails to fall to 100 beats per minute or less at ten minutes post-exercise.

Reduction of heart rate at standard conditions of rest, exercise and recovery are reflective of a more efficient heart (145). It is logical to expect that a given condition of rest or activity should always require approximately the same cardiac output from time to time. Therefore, a reduced heart rate suggests an increased stroke volume (51). Stroke volume at a given task (including rest) is a function of strength of the heart muscle (myocardium). Training in a fashion requiring elevated cardiac activity affects the myocardium by causing an increase in the size of myocardial fibers (hypertrophy) and thereby increasing the strength of the myocardium. The stronger heart muscle wrings more blood from the chambers at each beat, and the heart needs beat less frequently to achieve a given output.

Myocardial hypertrophy and related phenomena are not the only effects of aerobic training upon the heart. Previously non-functioning capillaries in heart muscle expand and become useful, and new capillaries are generated to form collateral blood flow routes, thereby providing superior perfusion of the myocardium with freshly oxygenated blood (92). Reasoning seems to dictate that this adaptation at least partially explains the lowered incidence of heart attacks in physically active people such as our now rather well-trained 40-year-old (41,88,98).

Pulmonary diffusing capacity is an expression of how rapidly oxygen diffuses across the lung membranes into the blood. Rhythmic training has been seen to facilitate this diffusion (128), probably through increased blood flow through the lungs (14). Early indications of this type of alteration usually appear after two or three months of training, and are associated with the previously discussed elevation of cardiac output. Obviously, if the heart puts out more blood, more blood flows through the lungs.

Maximal oxygen uptake ($\dot{V}O_2$ max) is the amount of oxygen utilized during the heaviest exercise one can sustain. It is dependent upon quality of cardiac function, pulmonary diffusing capacity, oxygen carrying capacity of blood and the ability of muscles to extract oxygen. Since all underlying factors are stimulated by rhythmic training, our jogger can expect to experience a nice increment. An eight to ten percent increase in $\dot{V}O_2$ max within six or eight weeks of training is common (2,79,108,136), but magnitude of change is governed considerably by starting point. Large increases are more easily achieved by those who begin with a low $\dot{V}O_2$ max.

So, within a period of about two months, our jogging, weight-training friend may expect to note increases in muscular endurance, decreased heart rate at rest and at submaximal work, accelerated recovery of heart rate following exertion and a superior pick-up and delivery of oxygen from inspired air to working muscle.

A number of other quite important physiological changes occur in instances, such as depicted by our subject, where training has become an aspect of the life style, and has, in fact, continued for six months or more. Muscular strength continues to increase, provided that additional resistance is added to each exercise from time to time. In part, this is due to further muscle fiber hypertrophy, but following about six weeks of weight training the physiological aspect of the Disinhibition Theory is apparently activated as well. In such cases, it is believed that connective tissue is developed and encapsulates tiny receptors imbedded in the muscle-tendon junction, thereby shielding them from distortion. These receptors are always responsive to stretch and tension developed when the muscle contracts and responds to such stimuli by automatically signalling the muscle to cease development of additional tension. When connective tissue, created through training, accumulates and surrounds these receptors, they receive their stimulation at higher tensions and thus refrain from signalling for a stop until greater force has been generated. Much of the strength increment seen after six weeks or more of serious muscle training is thus due to this mechanism.

There is another physiological adaptation which also contributes to strength development. Training stimulates the endocrine glands to secrete more male hormones (145) which in turn facilitate muscle fiber hypertrophy (145). The female as well as the male will experience this alteration, although to a much lesser extent. Women need not fear for loss of femininity through training; neither need they expect to see muscle hypertrophy or strength increments equal to that demonstrated by most males.

Although body weight reductions may be experienced by our jogger in the first several months of training, they may be as much an outcome of dieting as they are of training, since those inclined to initiate one health regimen are usually of a mood to begin others, control of caloric intake being a popular option. However, continuous training for a year or more apparently alters the metabolism and gradual and very nearly permanent weight losses ensue. The jogger may find that he can discard his restrictive diet while desired weight is maintained. This may be an effect of a proliferation and enlargement of mitochondria, the tiny energy-releasing structures in muscle (51); thus trained muscle is rendered a superior energy-releasing tissue, contributing to maintenance of appropriate body weight. Training for muscular development then is an activity appropriate for both sexes.

Long-term training also tends to increase the blood volume (67). Since about the same amount of plasma is added as are cellular components, the constituency of the blood remains about the same (67). The larger plasma volume serves as a reservoir for water loss through perspiration during heavy exercise. The trained body is thus better able to cool itself over long work periods. Furthermore, water loss from the blood volume during exercise concentrates the blood (101), thereby increasing its oxygen carrying capacity per unit of volume.

It is believed that rhythmic training of long duration ultimately generates very extensive capillarization of skeletal muscle and of the myocaridum, granting the recipient of such phenomena additional muscular endurance and protection against heart disease (84,92).

Our jogging, weight-training friend who has been exercising for approximately two months is now enjoying the benefits of increased oxygen uptake and physical working capacity, and a reduced heart rate at rest, as well as during exercise. Nevertheless, he is always careful to begin each training session with stretching exercises which prepare his body for the task at hand. The lengthening of the muscle tissue that results from positions held for 30 to 60 seconds is all-important to ensuing performance in that it increases blood flow to those specific muscles needed for jogging, gently stresses tendons and ligaments in preparation for forceful contractions and generally protects against injury.

The large muscles comprising the mass of tissue at the back of the upper leg (hamstring group) can be stretched by standing with feet about shoulder width apart and bending forward at the waist with arms hanging loosely in a position where discomfort is not a factor. It is rather a "toe-touch" position, although no effort is made to touch the toes. This position is held the usual 30 to 60 seconds. It is superior to the toe-touch because it does not generate a stretch reflex in the hamstring that is resistant to the held position.

The quadriceps are found on the front of the thigh. To stretch them, kneel on the ground with toes extended and heels spread apart. Flex the knees and drop the bottom so that, in effect, a seated position is assumed. Place the hands on the ground and lean back. Flex the elbows a bit until stretch is noticeable on top of the feet, front of upper and lower legs and in the abdomen. Hold the position. Never go to a point of pain. Each day will find a greater range of motion. Eventually one should be able to go all the way back until the shoulders touch the ground.

The large tendon that attaches calf muscles (soleus and gastrocnemius) to the heel must be stretched also. To neglect this area is to challenge an exquisitely painful condition in which the tendon becomes inflamed (Achilles Tendonitis). The hands are placed on a supportive object or structure and, with body rigid, the feet are backed away a bit at a time. Heels are kept in contact with the ground. The position is held when gentle stretching can be felt in the calf. This may also be done one leg at a time, if desired.

Relaxed trunk rotation done with feet spread wide will serve to stretch and relax hips and lower back. Five rotations in each direction is advised.

Large, loose arm-circles backward and forward may well prevent cramping sensations in the shoulders or "side-stitches" (cramps of the diaphragm) while jogging. Ten large arm-circles in each direction will suffice and they tend to retain range of motion in the shoulder girdle.

Stretching exercises should always be done smoothly without bobbing or vigorous, balistic movements. They serve as a useful aspect of warm-up, and those that stretch the legs should be repeated a time or two following a jog or run. After stretching, but prior to jogging, a brisk walk of about one-quarter mile, making certain to stride out long, will complete the warm-up. A similar walk will assure an uneventful cool-down period when done after the run, and serve to reduce likelihood of subsequent muscle stiffness or soreness.

Our jogger, now having persevered for several years, finds himself lean without special efforts at dieting, sinewy and strong for his size, capable of prolonged physical activity, durable also on the job and last, but by no means least, confident and certain of himself (69). Is it all worth it? Is it worth the time, the self-discipline, the energy, the effort, the discomfort? Ask the one who tried it.

SUGGESTED READING

Jokl, E. and Jokl, P., *The Physiological Basis of Athletic Records.* Springfield, Ill.: Charles C. Thomas, Publisher, 1968. Pp. xvi + 147.

Shephard, R. J., *Endurance Fitness.* Toronto: University of Toronto Press, 1969. Pp. ix + 246.

Astrand, P. O. and Rodahl, K., *Textbook of Work Physiology* (2nd ed.). New York: McGraw-Hill Book Co., 1977. Pp. xxi + 681.

Strauss, R. H., *Sports Medicine and Physiology.* Philadelphia: W. B. Saunders Co., 1979. Pp. xii + 441.

Chapter Seven

Ladies In Our Midst

Distance running and jogging are two areas of physical endeavor in which the human female can challenge the male. Furthermore, women realize the fact and are justifiably proud of it. One can expect that about every fifth jogger seen will be a woman. Practically every man has had the experience of starting a road race and discovering that some women can beat him, sometimes handily. No one can deny, however, that women and men are different. For example, women have a few distinct variations from men with regard to their response to training.

Let's begin with the gynocological aspect of training. Is menstruation really a factor? It most likely is not, except for the pain that some women experience. Dr. Tenley Albright (4), a former Olympic athlete and presently a practicing surgeon in Boston, advocates fitness and exercise as treatment for painful menstruation (dysmenorrhea). Cessation of periods (amenorrhea) has occurred in some athletes with extremely rigorous training. However, the periods resumed after training was altered (25).

A regular cycle is typical in athletes and has little effect on performance. A well-known study was made of more than 700 Hungarian women athletes who were asked about sport performance during the menstrual cycle (40). Nearly 50% declared there was no change; 30% felt a decrease in levels of performance and 13-15% experienced improved performance during the menstrual cycle. Perhaps improvement sounds a bit strange but we know that during the Tokyo Olympics four world records were set by girls who were menstruating.

The Pill has been utilized by some athletes to regulate the period to suit an athletic event. The cost for convenience, however, may have been the sacrifice of some level of performance. One study that was conducted to measure the influence of the Pill on performance found an increase in resting blood pressure and decreases in physical working capacity and maximal oxygen uptake (125).

An easier pregnancy and childbirth are typical of the physically active female. Pregnancy is a period of physical conditioning because of the increased demands upon metabolism and upon the entire cardiovascular system. Physically active women generally experience fewer incidences of complications during pregnancy, fewer cesarean sections, shorter durations of labor, faster deliveries and easier recoveries during the postpartum period. It is generally accepted that active women are better equipped to cope with labor because of the firm musculature of the abdomen and pelvic floor.

What levels of activity can be safely enjoyed during the various stages of pregnancy and subsequent breast-feeding? A rather well-known study by Dr. Rudolph Dressendorfer (38) of the Adult Fitness Program at the University of California involved a nonathletic young woman 27 years of age. She started a training program which consisted exclusively of slow distance running — 8-12 minute miles.

The subject began a jogging program in which weekly training mileage progressively increased from about ten miles initially to 35 miles. She continued to increase the work load to 50 miles per week, then became pregnant. Training mileage dropped to only five to ten miles per week in the first trimester because she experienced nausea and lassitude that persisted throughout the day. Thereafter, she was able to average about 15 miles per week up to delivery. Every two and one half months the subject was measured for maximal oxygen uptake ($\dot{V}O_2$ max) with the last measure taken four days prior to delivery. As performance improved as evidenced by greater distances covered throughout pregnancy, the expected increases in $\dot{V}O_2$ max were also observed. Ten days after delivery she was measured for $\dot{V}O_2$ max and values were nearly identical with those taken four days prior to delivery. Childbirth had little effect on $\dot{V}O_2$ max.

Training was resumed and testing continued during nursing, the primary source of infant nutrition. Throughout the investigation, no abnormal changes occurred. Routine examinations by an obstetrician and a pediatrician indicated that all clinical aspects of pregnancy, parturition and lactation were normal. The subject remained healthy throughout the investigation; pregnancy was normal and uncomplicated. Milk production during lactation was not noticeably affected by the high caloric cost and fluid losses inherent with long-distance runs of six to 18 miles.

A similar study has been recently reported — one involving 31 Finnish nonathletic women who trained during pregnancy in which the physical training had no disturbing effect on the course of pregnancy (38).

These findings may not apply to all pregnant or lactating women. However, many women who are healthy and physically active are likely to have a similar tolerance tor strenuous exercise. Perhaps during pregnancy it would be unwise for one to participate in field hockey or gymnastics or diving. However, there are many suitable activities — swimming, jogging or cycling.

Always in the past, the wisdom of jogging during pregnancy has been questioned. All of the Finnish women enjoyed normal progress as they continued their usual training programs. However, each individual should have her physician's approval. A jogging gynecologist who is knowledgeable concerning the benefits of exercise should be consulted.

Menstruation, pregnancy and lactation are obvious factors related to training that are unique to the female. There are other considerations.

Muscle mass in the female is less than in the male while percent of body fat is greater (90). However, it has been suggested that the latter may be an asset for endurance events. For any effort longer than 30 minutes, the body may turn to fat for fuel.

Woman is smaller than man, which is a negative factor in activities where size is important, such as basketball and football. This condition could be a real disadvantage to the female who wishes to play football or professional basketball. Contact sports played against males should be discouraged for most women in the interest of safety.

The female has a lighter bone structure with shorter long bones and hyperextended elbows and knees (96). The knee hyperextension provides poor support but is a definite asset in swimming. Females have weaker tendon attachments also, and therefore, the greater likelihood to have tendonitis and soreness. But women can probably approach certain male performances with practice and with greater numbers of women involved in athletics.

Hemoglobin concentration and red blood cell count are less in the female than in the male (51) but entirely adequate for the body size, as is the oxygen delivery system generally.

Lung size of the female is smaller than that of the male (51) and so, therefore, are two parameters which express the body's ability to move large amounts of air — maximal voluntary ventilation (MVV), the amount of air that can be moved in a 12 second period of time with rapid, deep breathing and forced vital capacity (FVC), the greatest volume of air that can be expelled by voluntary effort after a maximal inspiration, as well as pulmonary diffusing capacity (D_{LCO}), an expression of how rapidly oxygen diffuses across the lung membranes into the blood. However, all are appropriate to body size and not at all functionally inferior; simply different.

The heart is smaller in the female than in the male and therefore a greater heart rate is necessary for a given cardiac output. However, during heavy exercise there is less muscle tissue to require oxygenated blood.

In recent years physiologists have been reporting studies involving comparisons of female and male athletes. Rigorous training programs that are properly conducted enhance the health of women, who perform on a much more comparable basis with men than was previously thought possible (130). Efficiencies of both are similar during prolonged work.

Except for a difference in total body strength there is no significant biological inferiority.

Perhaps the reader has wondered how intensive training programs, such as swims of thousands of yards a day, affect young girls in regard to maturation. The young athlete's growth is facilitated by training (75). The female will mature earlier than her male counterpart, whether or not she trains. The training appears to have a very positive effect on the efficiency of all of the systems of the developing body (96).

Another difference between males and females may alleviate the concern of some women that they will develop masculine-looking legs with too much jogging. Androgens, or male hormones, do increase with training, even in females, and muscle hypertrophy will increase with increased androgen levels (90). However, it just isn't possible for the average woman to attain androgen levels that are equal to that of most men. Therefore, women need not worry about untoward increases in muscle mass; they do not have the hormonal potential.

If the musculature of any part of the body is ignored it will be soft and shapeless. With exercise it can become firm and shapely and exhibit the slight bit of tension that's known as muscle tone. Surely such an arm or leg — one that is firm with a slight curvature — if far more attractive than one that is soft and without shape!

32

Basal metabolism, i.e., operation of all the systems of the resting body, is lower in the female than in the male (51). The female will usually show a higher heart rate at a given work load than the male, and women generally have more difficulty with weight control than do men. This problem can be controlled in the most successful way by combining a good training program of exercise with a sensible diet that spreads calories over three or more small meals a day. With this combination one can enjoy not only the desired weight loss but also an optimal body composition (73). Metabolism remains elevated for several hours following exercise (134), another facet of training as an aid to weight control. The combination of diet and exercise not only supports the effort to lose weight and attain the optimal body composition, but appears to be the method of choice for maintaining that weight loss.

Concerning thermal adaptation — the female does not adapt to heat as well as does her male counterpart (39). However, she seems to adjust to the cold better. So don't avoid the cold. Jogging in the cold aids weight loss because it actually demands a higher energy cost (102).

The female is said to have a higher pain threshold than does the male. Perhaps this is why women are designed to bear babies. The ability to endure pain is a requisite for training, a plus for the female. As a matter of fact, this factor may well explain the observation that women more closely approach men in performance of endurance activities than in sprints.

The $\dot{V}O_2$ max is less in the female than it is in the male (90). But, like muscle mass and blood volume, it is entirely appropriate for body size.

The female athlete apparently reaches a performance peak sooner than does the male (145). Perhaps this is because she usually terminates her athletic career quite early in life. This causes one to wonder if some of these differences aren't social in nature. Indeed, female evolution may be socially imposed. A female athlete whose performance is superior to that of her peers may be a bit unpopular; unwanted even. Therefore, she hides her talent and cycles out, preferring the good will of the crowd. But . . . times are changing! Men are growing to realize that health and fitness are synonymous with beauty. Furthermore, women are beginning to care less about what men think. Modern women are active physically for themselves. That's as it should be. If others find female fitness attractive, so much the better.

In summary, the female response to exercise and training in many ways is similar to that of the male. However, frequently the magnitude of change varies between the sexes. For instance, as previously metioned, resistance training precipitates strength increments in the male and female alike; however, the amount of strength demonstrated by women is less than that by men. This is no doubt traceable to the fact that androgens stimulate hypertrophy, and these male hormones, of course, are in greater concentration in the male than in the female. For these reasons it is most unlikely that the female will challenge the male in power events. She is much more apt to rival him in activities that require endurance.

Maximal oxygen uptake probably best reflects endurance capability. Many studies have shown this parameter to be greater in men than in women, even when expressed per unit of body size. This disparity, however, is not likely to explain differences in endurance performance between the sexes, since the smaller maximal oxygen uptake observed in the female is in proportion to her lean body mass. In other words, the oxygen uptake is adequate to service the active tissue.

Other sex differences exist, as well. For instance, the heart rate at any given cardiac output (amount of blood pumped by the heart per minute) is greater in the woman than in the man. This apparent relative cardiac inefficiency is due to the woman's smaller heart, cardiac size being dictated by size of the thorax. In spite of this condition, endurance performance by the female is not thought to be inhibited by heart size. The female's heart is proportional to her body size and lean body mass; she is inclined to require a smaller cardiac output for a given work load than is the male, since she has a smaller "engine" to supply with oxygen and nutrient substances. To test this hypothesis, when jogging with a mixed group at an identical pace, derive the mean heart rate for females and males and you are likely to find no significant difference, even though the smaller females require smaller cardiac outputs for the same work loads.

It has been advanced that women may have an advantage in endurance events because of their higher percentage of body fat. Theory has it that since free fatty acids (FFA) are preferred as an energy source for long-term activity, the female will be favored since she has larger stores of triglyceride fats, which can be broken down to FFA and delivered to the muscle. In response to this it must be noted that even an extremely lean male marathoner, less than 5% body fat, has approximately 30,000 large calories (LC) stored on his body in the form of triglyceride fat. Yet he requires only 3,000 to 3,500 of those LC to run a two and one-half hour marathon. Thus it would seem that excess fat in the female just goes along for the ride.

Cardiac output and pulmonary diffusing capacity, as well as $\dot{V}O_2$ max, have been measured in the female and are known to be smaller than in the male. This evident deficiency is not likely to be restrictive to endurance performance since the parameters are in proportion to body size.

What, then, separates male and female performance? In the case of power activities (track sprinting, swim sprinting, weight lifting, putting the shot, throwing the discus and javelin, high jumping, pole vaulting and long jumping) the difference is strength. The female cannot hope to excel relative to the male in such events, since her genetic history has denied her the muscle mass required. This is not to say that some women cannot run a faster 100 meters than some men, since, obviously, there are overlaps in such considerations as body size, lean body mass and state of training. But, in your lifetime and mine, we need not expect to see a world record in a power event for women to excel that for men.

What about endurance events? An examination of world records will show that women more nearly approximate male effort in distance competition. The current record for swimming the English Channel both ways is held by a woman. Women's times for 1500 meters freestyle swimming are, percentagewise, closer to the male performance than they are in 100, 200 and 500 meters. It is not uncommon in an event such as the New York Marathon for the first woman across the finish line to have defeated thousands of men. In the world-famous Vassalopet, an 80 kilometer ski race in Sweden, many males were embarrassed in 1979, the first year for legal female participation, when several women finished in the top one hundred. This race attracts approximately 20,000 participants. The race originated about 400 years ago when the Swedish king, Erik Vassa, escaped his Danish captors and raced from Sälen to Mora, the existing race course, to rally the Swedish army. Vassa made the trip in about 12 hours and assumed heroic proportions for that feat. Today many women have beaten his time, by several hours! It's an extremely vigorous effort, and the women can make it and place well!

Why, then, haven't women set numerous records in endurance events that transcend sexual barriers? The reason, simply stated, is "Women ARE what they ARE because of what they've been for so long." Sociology, especially in western civilization, is such that female competitiveness is discouraged. Who knows how many women of the past bemoaned their strong limbs and hid their power under voluminous skirts? Haven't we all known girls who excelled at sport in elementary school, but later in their educational careers altered their participation in sport to conform with the prevalent social view of 'femaleness'! Imagine the pain suffered by a young girl six feet tall and 160 pounds who could throw a javelin farther than most men but was ostracized for being masculine!

Women's records in swimming and running events are improving at a rate far in excess of that for males, the reason being that only recently have women been encouraged to excel. There are many who believe that one day soon a woman will win a major marathon and that some other woman will be ranked among the top ten 1500 meter swimmers, regardless of sex.

It is always interesting, and frequently profitable, to look backward in time. Dickensian women were incomplete in attire without 20 petticoats and a bustle. This, by the way, was the only acceptable tennis costume at the time. The apparent need for such apparel was to protect the woman from the elements, but served effectively to inhibit her activity. In the same vein, menstruation was considered an illness; when the Victorian lady menstruated she was said to be unwell, which is an improvement over the Biblical description of "unclean." When pregnant, the nineteenth century impending mother expected a "laying-in" term, at which time complete bed rest was the custom. Today we know that exercising during menstrual flow is harmless in normal women, and may even alleviate the occasional accompanying discomfort. As mentioned earlier, studies have shown that Olympic gold medals have been won during all phases of the menstrual cycle. Evidently, although some women suffer unpleasant symptoms, menstruation is generally not inhibiting to quality of performance.

The more physiologically fit woman generally experiences fewer of the common female complaints — menstrual discomfort, backaches, digestive disorders, colds and especially fatigue. These common complaints among women of all ages — even the very young — are often the result of a lack of fitness. However, this problem is infrequently diagnosed as just that, and seldom given therapeutic attention.

As has been discussed, continued endurance training through

pregnancy is not only harmless but very possibly beneficial to the expectant mother (38). This finding has apparently been well-known in the Korean culture for some time, where it is customary for a mother to work in the rice field until the child is literally dropped. Upon this event the newborn is wrapped in warm cloth and, after a brief rest, we're told the mother returns to work.

One European study (40) presents data illustrating that the active female is much more inclined to have an uneventful pregnancy and presentation than is her sedentary counterpart. This study is especially important in view of the fact that a large number (about 700) of active and sedentary women were examined. Again, less sophisticated cultures would find it humorous that such exacting, scientific endeavor is required to reveal this fact. Many physicians in this country, however, are reluctant to prescribe, or even recommend, continued activity during pregnancy since there are indeed some who can be jeapordized.

A particular problem for the female who either reaches natural menopause or otherwise loses function of her ovaries is osteoporosis, a loss of structural strength of bone, particularly of the spinal column. Of course, hormone replacement therapy and dietary regimen play a major role in the treatment of this pathology. However, there is a strong possibility that stimulation of the skeletal system, by means of muscular contraction, i.e., physical activity, stimulates bone to retain its compact tissue. Conceivably, the menopausal female can retain normal skeletal structure and function, at least in part, by means of habitually taken physical exercise.

The body is a machine, and machines are meant to be used. Disuse destroys machines. Woman, and man, too, for that matter, can only gain by using the body for the purposes for which it was designed. I don't believe God really intended woman for the pedestal.

SUGGESTED READING

Dressendorfer, Rudolph H. and Goodlin, Robert C., Fetal heart rate response to maternal exercise testing. *The Physician and Sportsmedicine*, 8:91-96, 1980.

Gendel, E. S., Fitness and fatigue in the female. *Journal of Health, Physical Education and Recreation*, October: 53-58, 1971.

Huey, Lynda, *A Running Start*. New York: Quadrangle/The New York Times Book Co., 1976. Pp. xvi + 241.

Smith, E. L., Jr., Reddan, W. and Smith, P. E., Physical activity and calcium modalities for bone mineral increase in aged women. *Medicine and Science in Sports and Exercise*, 13:60-64, 1981.

Ullyot, Joan, *Women's Running.* Mountain View, CA: World Pulications, 1976. Pp. 155.

Chapter Eight

How Young Is Too Young And How Old Is Too Old

Is there an optimal age to begin training? Can one initiate physical training too early in life? These are questions of critical importance, in view of today's common practice of training the child in preparation for serious athletic competition. Unfortunately, there cannot be a single definitive answer — an age, or a yes or a no. Much depends on the nature of the training and, to some extent, upon the participant.

Probably because of their early appearance and national appeal, baseball and football have been rather well researched in regard to their suitability as training and competitive media for the child (52,70,74,95). In general, contact, such as in football, comes poorly recommended. Fractures of long bones during growth periods can be crippling (33,89,115). However, one would guess that such injuries would be even more commonplace in "sandlot" games played with neither proper supervision nor equipment. The child determined to play football is probably safer in a controlled, organized situation than in one in which broken bottles, tin cans, larger or older players and no enforcement of rules are everyday hazards.

Little League baseball appears to offer fewer risks to the young player than does football. However, the pitcher is inclined to develop serious elbow and shoulder problems and probably the curve ball should not be thrown until maturation is complete (52,89,115). Also, variations in maturational status among players in the absence of any within-league size divisions is dangerous. The immature batter finds it difficult to judge the fastball thrown the short distance from mound to plate by the considerably more mature pitcher. Furthermore, since this described situation is advantageous to winning, the most mature boy very often becomes the pitcher. One should also realize that little definitive study has been aimed at ascertaining cardiovascular and respiratory outcomes of participation by children in team sports, nor have we firm data regarding psychological effects.

Perhaps the most demanding of the child training regimens is directed at the swimmer. Age-group swimming, sponsored by the Amateur Athletic Union (AAU), has a history of a quarter-century. World-class swimming performances by youngsters in their teens have come to be accepted as commonplace. As I write these words, I am at poolside observing an age-group meet. There are slightly more than 1,000 children here. Age-groups in Florida are 8 and under, 9-10, 11-12, 13-14 and 15-18. In some states there is no 8 and under category; in others, there is not only an opportunity to compete in 8 and under, but as a 6 and under as well. It is not unusual to see six-year-old youngsters, and sometimes a few even younger, competing seriously in races. It must be realized that this is, indeed, serious competition with very careful preparation. Most age-groupers practice twice a day, five or six days weekly and cover as much as 10,000 meters per session. Twelve-year-old girls now swim better times than their college-age dads of twenty years ago. Presently in this country there is a growing AAU age-group track movement with similar rigorous training programs likely to evolve. And what accrues to the children as an outcome of such intense training? Are we destroying them? Are we creating monsters?

Obviously, training for competitive swimming is largely training of heart, lungs and blood vessels. Research, therefore, has looked at how the function of those organs changes with training. And has this rigorous training proved deleterious to the training children? On the contrary, studies have shown young swimmers and track athletes to have increased capabilities to extract oxygen from breathed air and deliver it to working muscle tissue (34,36,142), facilitated ability to send respiratory gases across membranes in the lungs and into the blood (131,137, 140), elevated ability of the heart to pump blood during exercise (9,94,124), increased ability to do physical work (12,34, 132) and increased muscular strength (15). Additionally, no basic differencies in nature of response to training have been noted between male and female children (142). Although data are not strong, there are some early indications that children involved in intense training for competitive swimming experience have no psychological harm as a result (69). Perhaps most important, to date no one has reported detrimental outcomes of hard cardio-respiratory or aerobic training of children.

It certainly appears that training to benefit heart, lungs and blood vessels cannot begin too early. In all probability, periods of systematic exercise should start within days of birth. After all, the function of the body is, primarily, movement. It is difficult to imagine how one might damage the organism by providing for its natural function. The argument that the child can be forced to do too much is an unlikely one in view of how much the kid swimmers do with only benefit to show for the effort. And, any swim coach will tell you that it is impossible to make a tired child do more. Children are self-regulating! Perhaps if coach insists upon one more lap, the youngster will do it, but in a most untaxing manner.

We make a plea here to parents to encourage physical activity rather than to "protect" the child from it. If such activity were unhealthful, scientific research, by this time, would have identified it. If your child is normal (and most children are), he cannot be physiologically damaged by something as natural as exercise.

What about "athlete's heart?" Isn't it true that the heart enlarges as an outcome of physical training and after the athletic career is terminated, doesn't it "turn to fat" and lose its function? These are questions of ancient heritage. They have long been asked, and they continue to be asked. The heart does in fact become larger with training designed to increase cardiorespiratory endurance. This is a normal, healthful phenomenon. It encourages efficiency of cardiac function. Upon cessation of training, much of this muscle hypertrophy of cardiac muscle is lost. The muscle can no more change to fat than can a metaphysicist convert lead to gold. The lost function is a genuine loss and reduces the ability of the heart to pump blood, especially during exercise. However, the fact of loss of cardiac efficiency upon cessation of training is a valid argument for continuation of training, not for avoidance of training initially.

How does the child athlete fare in later life? Unfortunately, few data exist in this area presently. It is known, though, that what one does presently is more important than what one did years ago (37,49). This is best exemplified by the scientific observation that athletes who continue to train into later life continue also to physiologically outperform their sedentary counterparts (106, 107,111,118). Although team sport athletes often have difficulty continuing with their activity, it is hoped that early training might lead to appreciation of superior physical status with a resulting continued participation in some form of vigorous activity. Whether or not this actually happens is not established.

Much has been said about adverse psychological effects on children of intense competition or of exposure to certain types of adults associated with children's athletic's programs. It seems rather likely that such outcomes are possible, but accurate measurement in this area is difficult. That a child might be damaged by experiences connected with sport is frightening and regrettable. However, we must point out that it is not the activity that is at fault but rather artificial conditions structured by non-participants.

An objective view of the scientific literature clearly shows that there is much for the child to gain through early involvement in aerobic training, and at the very least, it strongly suggests that, barring contact or unusual repetitive movements, training the normal child does no harm. When the training begins apparently is not critical, unless one wishes to consider that an early start is best. Since swimming relieves the skeletal system of the need to support body weight, this activity may well be best for developing aerobic capacity in children because the possibility of joint damage is reduced.

But perhaps there is a time when one is too old to train. Our customs dictate that this is so. We all have difficulty imagining our grandparents jogging. There are many reports indicating favorable training outcomes for middle-aged men (48,49,79, 128) and women (86,87). Continued training past seventy years of age has been shown to maintain superior physiological function (135). Those middle-aged and even older who have experienced heart disease have been observed to recover close to 100 percent of original function through aerobic training (80,83, 92). Occasionally, unfounded derogatory articles appear in the popular literature, but scientific endeavor has failed to uncover any adverse effects of reasonably conducted aerobic training upon heart, lungs and blood vessels, regardless of age of participants, except in cases where significant abnormalities existed prior to beginning the exercise.

If one's bodily equipment is without major flaw, training can be initiated in middle years or later with expectations of healthful improvements. A caution for the older athlete; contrary to popular practice, medical input and practical guidance are required when beginning a training program. If physical activity has not been an aspect of the lifestyle for years there may well be hidden factors that eliminate participation or reduce its allowable intensity. A physician *must* be consulted. Furthermore, as natural as walking and jogging may seem, there are right and wrong ways to do these things, and there are correct as well as faulty ways to progress in training, regardless of mode. The beginner needs advice. Both whether or not to begin and definition of beginning intensity are functions of the physician. If he cannot take the next step and plan the program one may apply to the YMCA or the local hospitals, some of which sponsor fitness programs. Should these measures fail, ask a jogger to identify the local "jogging doc." There seems to be such a physician in every community. Seeing him will be money well spent.

When to begin? Immediately, if not sooner! There is no "too early" and, as long as you live, no "too late."

SUGGESTED READING

Burke, E. J. (ed.), *Toward an Understanding of Human Performance*. Ithaca, NY: Mouvement Publications, 1977. Pp. iv + 92.

Sidney, K. H. and Shephard, R. J. Frequency and intensity of exercise training for elderly subjects. *Medicine and Science in Sports*, 10:125-131. 1978.

Chapter Nine

How Much Is Enough And How Much Is Too Much

Part I

After considerable rummaging in the closet, Clyde succeeded in locating his old high school physical education shorts. Lord, they seemed small! The emblem on the right leg read, "West Wockington Falls H.S. — Phys. Ed." "Fizz ed," mused old, fat Clyde, "Sounds like a new cola drink." With some effort he managed to work the shorts up over his buttocks, but the belly was a different problem. Gazing downward in some dismay Clyde could observe hopeless masses of fat tumbling over the elastic band of the shorts. "Dunlop's Disease," he thought. "My stomach done lops over my pants."

Now for the shoes. Once upon a time, Clyde could clearly recall, there had been an abortive attempt at tennis and he'd purchased tennis shoes. Somewhere in all this disarray those neat, white rascals were hiding. Clyde was tiring of this. His face was red and he could feel his heart pounding. "Damn, where *are* they?" More snorting, picking and rummaging. No luck. But what is this? The old Army boots! What memories they brought back — 20 mile hikes — double-timing it for a mile or more with full pack — that girl in Berlin who could — well, never mind. On with the boots. Lace 'em up. Clump about the room a bit. Trifle tight. Much heavier than they used to be, it seemed. Well, they'll do.

Clyde, in all his glory, marched to the front door and pushed it open. Purposely, this late hour had been chosen. Darkness would conceal his efforts until a few pounds were shed. Now a big breath — someone had told Clyde that was a good thing to do before jogging. "In with the good air," he murmured "and out with the bad (wheeze)." Suddenly Clyde felt old, fat and tired. Maybe tomorrow would be better. "No!" Clyde spoke the word aloud, then glanced about to see if the sound had attracted attention. An audience had not materialized. A moment of most unusual resolve seized him — and Clyde bolted out the door. "One mile," he gritted, "as fast as I can go!"

The first few yards felt good. Clyde recalled his university days when, with minimal training, he had represented his fraternity as a miler in the intramural track meet. Even now he could remember his brothers cheering him on — "Go, Clyde, go!" — perhaps the most cherished few minutes of his life. Clyde the athlete — admired — running smoothly — gracefully. The memory spurred him on. Head held high, arms swinging powerfully, Clyde covered the first 200 yards in grand style. But the shoes were growing heavy, and pinching uncomfortably. The traffic light at the intersection, one-half mile from home, glimmered in the distance. "Well," Clyde thought, "pain is part of it. No pain, no progress. Come on feet!" A quarter mile gone, and the pace, if anything, had picked up. Clyde was paying the price, but admiring himself for such self-discipline. "After a few days," he told himself, "this will be a snap."

Now to the light — don't stop! Don't stop! Clyce circumscribed a teetering circle on the narrow sidewalk and began to retrace his steps, "My God — that much again to go!" Breath came in gasps now. Where was that second wind? Could that twinkle so far away really be the porch light? Must be — everyone else asleep. Something searing hot seemed to grasp Clyde's right side and a groan harmonized with the gasp of breathing. "Side-stitch," muttered the runner, "damn!" A good excuse to stop. The porch light glimmered like a pot of gold at the end of a hopelessly long rainbow. "Never! I can do it!" He pounded on heavily, no longer concerned about grace or smoothness, oblivious to the echoing sound of his tread.

Clyde stumbled over — what? A leaf? A twig? A long stride saved a fall but produced a warm, uncomfortable feeling in the groin. "What the hell is one more pain," thought Clyde, now conscious of two things: he was hot and he was not perspiring. Everything felt dry, right down to his feet. A determined smile spread over the pale face, "If I were in real bad shape," went the thought, "I'd be sweatin' my fanny off. I can make it!" He imagined again the cheers of his fraternity brothers and made the huge effort required to lift the feet and control the staggering. Each breath felt hot now — searing to the lungs, "Move, move, move!" Arms now hanging loosely. Approaching the porch. One more breath! One more stride! Clyde almost fell, and this time he knew the stumbling block — nothing. Trembling hand

45

on the porch rail. "You made it. Baby — you made it! Ran every step of the way. Wonder how fast? Must time it tomorrow." Long gasping shudders served as breathing. He was dizzy and had the sensation that he was looking down a long tunnel. His head pounded. A wave of nausea completely inundated Clyde; he turned and vomited into the shrubbery, trying desperately to quiet the retching. "Please, don't let anyone hear," prayed the miserable athlete, mortified at his weakness.

The vomiting seemed to make him feel better. Unsteadily he made his way into the house, showered — lots of steaming water over complaining muscles and joints — crawled into bed quietly so as not to disturb Mrs. Clyde. "I'll sleep well tonight," he thought. And he did.

The electric buzz of the alarm was as rude as ever. Clyde popped open his eyes and rolled toward the clock. *Tried* to roll toward the clock. Pain shot over his body like a lightening bolt, eliciting a gasp which, in turn, produced a staggering pain in Clyde's chest, a penetrating stab that now accompanied each breath. "Dear God, I'm having a heart attack! I'm dying!" Clyde turned wildly rotating eyes toward his wife. He could not speak — he could barely breathe. Mrs. Clyde slept soundly. "Must get up — telephone." One leg out of bed. Pain unbearable. Raise the trunk. Pain. Awful Pain, reaching to the genitals. Falling, falling, falling. Crash. "I'm dead," Clyde remembers thinking that.

"Well, now. It seems heaven is all white and blurry." Clyde blinked in an effort to clear his vision. Voices alternately blared and faded. Was that his wife speaking?

"He'll be all right," commented Dr. Zorch. "I can't imagine how he managed it, but he has severely irritated the proximal end of the trachea — the windpipe — and that causes the pain with breathing. The edema — fluid at knees and ankles — contributes to the generalized pain as does a stretched inguinal ligament. If I didn't know Clyde better, I'd swear he'd exercised violently. You two didn't have a knock-down, drag-out, did you?" He smiled encouragingly at Mrs. Clyde, trying to erase the worry from the tear-stained face.

Clyde closed his eyes. "I don't ever want to face this," he considered, and for an instant wished he had indeed died.

It seems that Clyde over did.

Part II

Jim swallowed the last of his six ounces of Gatorade, checked the tightness of his shoe laces and continued with the remain-

46

ing minutes of his half-hour of stretching exercises. The marathon distance had years ago ceased to terrorize him, but this race was important to him since it fell on his 50th birthday and he hoped to run his best-ever time. Therefore, this careful planning, including the carbohydrate depletion run scheduled for today. After no carbohydrate ingestion to speak of for four days, and this twenty-mile run, he looked forward to four days of rest and unrestricted diet.

The first half-mile was always a chore. Jim felt stiff in spite of stretching, and awkward. He seemed to be breathing too heavily for the job at hand. Uncomfortable, but not distressing. In the experience of nineteen years of jogging and running, this was the usual first-mile condition. But the pace for the day was a problem. A depletion run is intended to nearly exhaust whatever muscle glycogen (carbohydrate) remains after hard training with little carbohydrate replacement. However, the marathon itself was only four days away. To push too hard would result in some muscle fiber wall damage, ultimately repaired to a superior condition by normal body processes, but likely to produce lingering soreness for several days. "Better listen to the old body," thought Jim, "and cut back a bit." He slowed the pace.

Mile two was pleasant. The sun, even at this early morning hour, was warm on the shoulders. Sweat glistened on the brow, neck and forearms. Jim estimated, again from experience, that his heart rate was in the neighborhood of 120 beats per minute. Respiration was easy now, and the legs felt great. As he grew older, legs more frequently became the stopper. When they let him down, there was no collapse; just an ache and an inability to move any faster than about an 8-minute mile pace. His best efforts came when the legs held up, and they had held up best after carbohydrate loading.

Jim's mind was wandering — thinking about other races — other training days — the theories supporting training practices. With a start he recognized the old water tower — nearly five miles from his beginning point. He had lost track of pace and with no time cues could do nothing to restructure it. He felt good — perhaps too good. "Probably too slow — pick it up a bit." An observer would have noticed a slightly lengthened stride.

It was a gorgeous morning. Drops of dew glistened on blades of grass like diamonds and the toe caps of Jim's running shoes grew damp. The sun was low on the eastern horizon with sufficient mist before it to appear as a shimmering orange fireball. Miasmas arose from water standing in the fields and from ponds where cattle watered. A stately white heron stalked through water in the roadside ditch searching for a green frog who had stayed out too late. The bird made a sudden stabbing movement and a wriggling something appeared magically in its bill. "Breakfast is served," murmured the runner. He had watched that drama scores of times when on long runs, always with fascination. Survival of the fittest. If there was a persisting natural truism, that was it. No matter how mankind progressed it seemed that in order to survive, one had to be fit for existing conditions. Jim thought of the many of his business and social acquaintances who had proved unfit and had failed — failed professionally or in marriage. Then there was the ultimate failure — death. The shock of his younger brother's death by heart attack haunted Jim. Charlie had so much to give. Maybe death wasn't failure. After all, everyone eventually did it. Perhaps . . . death marks the end of something, but also a beginning.

With a jolt Jim returned to reality from his mental meanderings. Glancing at familiar scenery he realized there were but six miles remaining in his run. "Run down the check list — legs: dull ache but good; breathing: deep, but regular and easy; arms: rather cramped; nausea, headache, dizziness: none. Truly, a nice run!" The remaining miles were downhill. Jim lengthened his stride and picked up the cadence. He felt good. Perspiration drenched him. His shorts were soaked. The headband would yield a half cup when squeezed out at the end of the twenty miles. "All systems are go! Let me feel this good on Saturday!"

Saturday came. And Saturday went. Three hours, twenty-nine minutes and some-odd seconds. Eleven minutes plus over his previous best. No personal record for a birthday gift this year. The first twenty had felt so good — it was the last six that proved impossible. Legs again. Just no get-up-and-go left. Jim arose from the brick wall surrounding the courthouse where he'd planted himself with a cool drink after some loose walking following his finish. Curiously he wandered toward the finish line and watched the stragglers come in. In a sense, each finisher was a winner — no one had run any farther. Nevertheless, Jim was disappointed. The depletion run and subsequent carbohydrate loading had failed. "Perhaps I under-did it — ."

Part III

How much is enough? It depends on the participant. The limits must be known. Heart rates must be established by some reliable system. In the beginning, walking (not jogging) less than a mile may be enough.

How much is too much? It depends on the participant. The limits must be known. Heart rates must be established by some reliable system. In the beginning, walking (not even jogging) less than a mile may be too much.

Pay attention to your body. Distress signals a need to terminate. There is no disgrace in walking home. Be aware that limits vary. Yesterday's work-out may be too much today. Aim first for 20 minutes of walking or jogging at a pace that maintains an appropriate heart rate. From there, decide if you want to be a 20-minute jogger, a marathoner, or something in between. Be aware that your goals will change. Whatever you do, don't pull a Clyde!

SUGGESTED READINGS

American College of Sports Medicine, *Guidelines for Graded Exercise Testing and Exercise Prescription*, (2nd ed.). Philadelphia: Lea and Febiger, 1980. Pp. xiii + 151.

American College of Sports Medicine, Position statement on the recommended quantity and quality of exercise for developing and maintaining fitness in healthy adults. *Sports Medicine Bulletin*, 13:1:3-4, 1978.

Fixx, J. F., *The Complete Book of Running*. New York: Random House, 1977. Pp. xxii + 314.

Fox, E. L., *Sports Physiology*. Philadelphia: W. B. Saunders Co., 1979. Pp. xi + 383.

Pollock, M. L., How much exercise is enough? *The Physician and Sports Medicine*, 6:1-11, 1978.

Chapter Ten

Theories of Fatigue

It may well be that, except for the search for the origins of life, the effort to identify the sources of fatigue represents the most intense and prolonged of all scientific endeavors. A century or two ago, the motivating force for such investigation was the plain fact that human muscle power provided most of the energy expended in industry and agriculture. Today, interest remains high due to the political importance attached to national sport excellence and to considerations related to impending space travel. Whatever the nature of the physical effort, fatigue precipitates cessation. One must know the enemy to effectively combat him. Prevention of fatigue is unlikely until its nature is understood.

Unfortunately, there appears to be about as many theories of fatigue as there are theorists. However, basically all major hypotheses fall into one of five categories: those which indict either the circulatory or respiratory systems, or both; those accusative of increasing body temperature; theories identifying dehydration as causative; those accusative of depletion or blockage of energy sources; psychological explanations. Some theories considerably overlap two or more of the basic categories but nevertheless can be assigned as predominantly one or another. Actually, in the final analysis, ability to continue work seems to be dependent upon the functional competence of muscle cells to release energy. Anything that obstructs this capability is representative of fatigue.

Oxidation is a process in which molecular oxygen (O_2) associates with some fuel in such a fashion that the potential energy in the fuel substance is released. A fire is an example of rapid oxidation. One effective means to control a fire is to regulate the amount of O_2 that reaches it. Obviously, a fire can be completely put out simply by shutting off its source of O_2. When one places a cover over the chimney of a candle lamp he does exactly that. The flame becomes smaller and dimmer as available O_2 is consumed, and finally, the flame dies. Since energy release in a cell is an oxidative process, it is easy to understand why early hypotheses suggested that failure of circulation or respiration might be the seat of fatigue. Exercise demands more energy. Energy substrate is available, and so, at first, is O_2. However, as exercise continues, this theory goes, circulation and respiration have more and more difficulty delivering oxygen to the contracting muscle. Depreciating ability to continue quality performance would be, in this theory, akin to the candle flame growing dimmer. Some credence is lent to this theory by the common observation that well-trained athletes — those with high resistance to fatigue — have significantly greater ability to consume oxygen (31,136), larger exercise cardiac outputs (94,124) and greater quantities of blood (67) than do normal but less active counterparts. However, research has also shown that even in fatigue there is plenty of O_2 in the blood returning to the lungs from active muscle (66). It is difficult to accuse the O_2 pick-up and delivery systems if the working muscle receives all the O_2 it can extract and more.

Delivering O_2 to working muscle is far from the entirety of circulatory and respiratory function. These systems must also dispose of cellular wastes. Such materials, if allowed to accumulate, can as surely put out the flame of oxidation as can O_2 elimination. Concentration of lactic acid ($H1^+$) in blood has been observed to rise with approaching fatigue (63), suggesting that the elimination function of the circulation could not keep up with waste formation. The blood $H1^+$ concentration is *always* elevated as fatigue approaches. It is a highly diffusible substance, however, and departs the muscle quickly in favor of the blood. Furthermore, one would suspect that a quite specific level of $H1^+$ in the blood would always be sufficient to put a stop to physical effort. Not only is blood $H1^+$ concentration extremely variable in fatigue from person to person, but an individual can increase his tolerance for $H1^+$ by appropriate training (103).

It has been reported that individuals fatigue when central body temperature reaches about 40°C (1,45,93). Although this data is limited, it gains credence due to the fact that the temperature was constant from time to time and from person to person. One would conceive that a temperature sensing mechanism shuts down exercise supporting systems when the appropriate temperature is reached, much as a thermostat closes down a furnace at a pre-set temperature. Also, this theory is supported by the practical observation that the onset of fatigue is facilitated by a hot environment.

51

The well-trained individual perspires profusely during prolonged activity. The water in perspiration is derived from blood plasma and tissue fluids. Loss of this water is known as dehydration. Excessive dehydration can cause systematic shock and loss of consciousness. It seems likely that some sort of safety mechanism would stop the performer short of these dire consequences and there is some evidence that such does occur. When the blood is volume depleted as a result of fluid loss through perspiration, a competition for remaining blood exists between the O_2 demanding musculature and the skin, where heat carried by blood from the core is passed to the environment. It seems that one of two eventualities will be brought about. Either the muscle gets the blood and exericse is halted by heat accumulation, or the skin gets the blood and exercise is stopped by O_2 shortage (ischemia) in the skeletal muscles.

Glycogen, an energy source in the muscle, has been observed to decrease dramatically during heavy exercise, and to be at about the same low concentration in different people at the point of fatigue (30,46,129). In addition, altering diet and training intensity has been shown to result in elevated muscle glycogen concentration and prolonged ability to do heavy work (13,62,78). Really, there is little doubt that increased availability of this important substrate can improve endurance performance. However, those skeptical that depreciated quantities of glycogen in working muscle explain fatigue, point out that there is some glycogen available to the muscle when it will no longer contract. The stores are evidently never fully depleted.

It has been reported that blood glucose concentration is low at fatigue (71), and this phenomenon has been accused as being causative of fatigue. The argument is that when the neural pathways responsible for carrying the message to contract to muscles have little blood sugar as an energy source, their function is obliterated. Thus, fatigue becomes a nervous system problem. The muscles fail to contract because they no longer get the message. The criticism of this theory is identical to that of depreciated muscle glycogen stores: blood glucose concentration never reaches zero.

Free fatty acids (FFA), mobilized from fat stores on the body, are important sources of energy for the endurance performer (28,64,104). There are about 50,000 kilocalories stored in the average man's body in the form of fat. A marathoner spends about 3,000 kilocalories during his race. Obviously, there is no shortage of this energy source. However, during prolonged heavy exercise $H1^+$ accumulates in the blood, and this substance obstructs mobilization of FFA from fat depots. It is possible that fatigue results when the performer demands energy from fat stores and finds that source blocked.

When one wants to protect the family automobile and those in it from the heavy-footed driver, an accelerator governor is placed on the carburetion system. To protect the machine, control the engine. Skeletal muscle is the engine of the body. It seems logical that a mechanism designed to protect the body as a whole would be housed in the muscle. However, neither energy substrate depletion nor $H1^+$ accumulation in the muscle appears to explain fatigue. It has been hypothesized that perhaps a breakdown in function of the muscle-contained cytochrome chain explains muscular fatigue. The cytochrome chain (or respiratory chain) passes hydrogen ions (H^+) along a chemical pathway to ultimately form $H1^+$. If the system fails, H^+ would accumulate, rendering the environment acid and unsuitable for further contraction. As nice a theory as this seems, research has shown the cytochrome chain to be entirely effective (77).

In Man, psychology no doubt plays an important role in development of fatigue. The human being interprets his condition and guesses about how long he can continue. Other animals probably don't do this, at least not to the same extent as does Man. Possibly, conditions existent in fatigued muscle tissue of lower animals are not evident in Man's. When maximal exercise testing is done in laboratories, subject declaration of fatigue is often accepted as true fatigue. Under laboratory conditions some individuals will push themselves to trembling nausea and near collapse; whereas, others will stop at the first sign of discomfort. Although no one disputes that training for endurance work will precipitate physiological changes that could conceivably function to delay onset of fatigue, it is very likely that a significant amount of the improved performance observed in trained athletes is due to an altered psychology that allows for a different interpretation of fatigue. When the athlete has pushed himself many times through fatigue to near exhaustion, he knows well the sensations that accompany such phenomena and knows also that somehow it is always possible to run one more stride or swim one more stroke.

These many possibilities seem only to cloud our understanding. Just what *is* fatigue? The most likely answer is that it is many things — different things in different people — even different things in the same person from time to time. Unfit individuals have been measured and found to be fatigued, by their own perception, after only five minutes of treadmill walking at 3.5 mph up a 5% grade. Subsequent to aerobic training the same subjects have been able to walk for as long as ten minutes at a 10% slope (128). Often young athletes cannot be brought to fatigue by treadmill walking regardless of slope, and must be run for such purposes, sometimes as fast as 9.0 mph at slopes exceeding 20% (140). When untrained, habitually sedentary humans declare fatigue, typically they have not perspired, but show signs of poor peripheral circulation as evidenced by pallor and cyanosis (blue coloration of lips, ear lobes, fingertips). They demonstrate heart rates of less than 150 bpm, and are not in acute respiratory distress. Why do they stop? Is it all psychological? Probably not. Were one to measure their central body temperatures, the critical 40°C has likely been approached. The blood volume in those sedentary is small and, during heavy exercise, most of it is required at the contracting muscle. The peripheral circulation is shut down and heat cannot be dissipated.

On the other hand, when endurance athletes declare fatigue during laboratory testing, they are drenched with perspiration, have heart rates frequently in excess of 200 bpm, exchange 100 liters of air per minute or more and usually show clear signs of excellent peripheral circulation. Is the reason these athletes stop entirely physiological? Probably not. At such heavy levels of duress, particularly when one is quite familiar with the symptoms, it all becomes a value judgment. Is it worth more to continue or to stop? The human inclination to interpret intervenes. The world champion endurance athlete is, more likely than not, the one who is most willing to put up with discomfort.

It is not against scientific rules to structure a workable theory on the basis of existing knowledge even though there are interruptions in the framework. Such a functional concept has been described (144) and is schematically represented on the next page.

This explanation is one which identifies depletion or blocking of energy sources as cause of fatigue. When blood sugar drops (hypoglycemia) the nervous system is deprived of its only energy source. Work stops, in a sense, in order that the nervous system may continue in all of its other very improtant integrative activities, such as regulation of circulation and respiration. Of course, psychological considerations can intervene at any of the above stages and cause cessation of work. In the untrained, it

54

SCHEMATIC —
THEORY OF FATIGUE

muscle glycogen used
O_2 deficit accrued

BEGIN WORK

$H1^+$ produced

hyperglycemia
glucose and FFA used

STEADY STATE

minimal $H1^+$ production

mild hypoglycemia
FFA used

APPROACHING FATIGUE

$H1^+$ production increased

moderate hypoglycemia
$H1^+$ blocks FFA mobilization

NEAR FATIGUE

blood glucose and muscle
glycogen used

severe hypoglycemia
nervous system deprived
of glucose

FATIGUE

work stops

may be that the subject's psyche interferes at the second or third phase. The athlete probably has no significant psychological intervention until he is quite near to "physiological fatigue." Furthermore, central body temperature might become a factor in some individuals prior to significant reduction of blood glucose. In particular, the untrained may be stopped by elevated temperature because of his inability to direct blood volume to the body surface.

Although this discussion cannot fully clarify the phenomenon of fatigue, it can provide insights into its probable nature. Absolute prevention of fatigue is not currently possible; it may never be possible. In the meantime, training appears to be the method of choice to delay onset of fatigue.

SUGGESTED READING

Bergstrom, J., Hermansen, L., Hultman, E. and Saltin, B., Diet, muscle glycogen and physical performance. *Acta Physiologica Scandinavica,* 71:140-150, 1967.

Fox, E. L. and Mathews, D. K., *The Physiological Basis of Physical Education and Athletics* (3rd ed.), Philadelphia: Saunders College Publishing, 1981. Pp. xvi + 677.

Hermansen, L., Hultman, E. and Saltin, B., Muscle glycogen during prolonged severe exercise. *Acta Physiologica Scandinavica,* 71:129-139, 1967.

Hickson, R. G., Rennie, M. J., Conlee, R. K., Winder, W. W. and Holloszy, J. O., Effects of increased plasma fatty acids on glycogen utilization and endurance. *Journal of Applied Physiology: Respiratory, Environmental and Exercise Physiology,* 43:829-833, 1977.

Issekutz, B., Jr., Issekutz, A. G. and Nash, D., Mobilization of energy sources in exercising dogs. *Journal of Applied Physiology,* 29:691-697, 1970.

Karlsson, J. and Saltin, B., Diet, muscle glycogen and endurance performance. *Journal of Applied Physiology,* 31:203-206, 1971.

MacDougall, J. D., Duncan, J., Reddan, W. G., Layton, C. R. and Dempsey, J. A., Effects of metabolic hyperthermia on performance during heavy prolonged exercise. *Journal of Applied Physiology,* 36:538-544, 1974.

Zauner, C. W. and Reese, E. G., Specific training, taper and fatigue. *Track Technique,* 49:1546-1550, 1972.

Chapter Eleven

What to Eat and Drink — and When

The athlete's diet has been an item of scientific and pseudo-scientific interest for centuries. No doubt, early man noted that starvation brought weakness and leaped from that observation to the conclusion that performance was influenced by what one ate. To acquire the courage of a lion, eat the flesh of a lion. With this consideration, it may no longer seem strange that Roman gladiators felt obliged to drink the warm blood of a young, vigorous bull prior to combat. This concept persisted until quite recent years as illustrated by the steak serving offered as a pre-game meal to American football players, a tradition still practiced by some.

When it became clear that food served as fuel for performance, implications for the athlete were again considered. What food substance was the best energy source? What aiding substances, such as vitamins and minerals, had to be supplied in abundance to enhance energy release? In terms of proximity to performance, when should the athlete eat? Should he eat solids or liquified substances?

Fat is the most concentrated energy source of all foods (51). On the surface, one would guess that this material is ideal for ingestion by the athlete, especially since muscle tissue appears to have a talent for using fats for energy release (28,64). However, fat requires more O_2 to release its energy than do other food materials (51). In heavy exercise, O_2 is at a premium and the more required by the contracting muscle, the less there is available for other critical functions. Furthermore, fats are absorbed from the small intestine into the lymph and from there mixed with venous blood in the right side of the heart. From that point they pass through the lungs where they obstruct O_2 transfer (126). Furthermore, fat loaded blood reduces O_2 transfer to the heart muscle (114). None of these things seem to indicate that fat is good for the athlete to ingest in preparation for physical activity, even though it is mobilized from fat stores on the body during prolonged exercise in a form that does not adversely affect transfer of the respiratory gases.

Muscle tissue is comprised of protein, which in turn is constructed of amino acids. Although supplementing the young athlete's diet with amino acids during intense muscle training may increase the rate of formation of new lean tissue (143), the idea that such substances supply energy is erroneous. Of all energy yielders, protein is the least likely to be utilized, simply because it is primarily found in muscle tissue. One does not dismantle the engine for better performance!

Ever since depreciating blood sugar levels were associated with onset of fatigue, carbohydrates have been seen as a logical substance to consume before physical performance. However, digestion and absorption rates are such that it is absolutely pointless to consume them immediately before the effort, even though they may be in the form of simple sugars. As a matter of fact, starting with sugars in the digestive system may lead to intestinal absorption of water from the plasma volume, magnifying a shortage precipitated by perspiring.

Consuming vitamins and minerals just before the gun is equally futile even though such substances are involved with the chemistry of cellular energy release. There simply isn't time for materials to pass through the stomach and to be absorbed from the intestinal tract. Furthermore, since their action is not in the blood, it is difficult to imagine that elevated levels of vitamins in the blood would enhance energy release or facilitate performance.

If it appears that arranging the diet for the physically active is an uncertain affair, the judgment is an accurate one. Some are on record as saying that a balanced diet is all the athlete requires (96). In the past this has been a safe statement and went unchallenged. Presently, however, there seems to be some concern regarding just how balanced the traditional balanced diet is. Even if such a diet is adequate for the athlete, can we be assured he will avail himself of it? Perhaps he isn't aware of what comprises a balanced diet, or cannot afford it — or simply won't eat it.

There seems to be little doubt that the athlete does need some special things. He requires more sleep than do those less active (117), and he certainly needs more exercise. Why is it logical to assume that his dietary needs do not differ from the rest of the population? In some instances, it appears ridiculous to assume similarity in dietary requirements. For example, since the athlete expends so many calories daily through training, he must have an increased caloric intake or fail to maintain his body weight. Also, since severe exercise is known to damage muscle fibers, thus necessitating repair, why is it logical to think that the active individual requires no more than the usual intake of amino acids? The in-training individual is really pretty much in the business of energy release. Does it seem proper to assume that he has no greater need for the vitamins required in the chemistry of such release? Finally, the endurance athlete transmits huge quantities of O_2 from lungs to metabolizing cells via the blood. Hemoglobin is the blood pigment which carries O_2. The more hemoglobin is concentrated in the blood, the greater the O_2 carrying capacity of the blood. Hemoglobin is comprised in part of iron. Adding iron in its proper form to the diet has been seen to favorably influence certain forms of anemia. Doesn't it appear likely that the athlete's diet ought to be rich in iron, particularly in the case of the female athlete who loses significant quantities of hemoglobin monthly through menstruation?

We believe the athlete has special dietary requirements. To begin with, unless weight loss is desired, he must take in enough calories to balance those he expends. Simply put, athletes must eat more than do sedentary individuals. Since body fat is inactive tissue and since even the leanest of athletes has tens of thousands of calories stored on the body as fat, this substance need only be in small evidence in the diet. Endurance effort is apparently heavily dependent upon stores of carbohydrate in muscle (13), and at least one theory identifies depressed concentration of blood glucose, a carbohydrate, as causative of fatigue (144). Thus, it seems correct to acquire the desired increased caloric intake primarily by means of carbohydrate. And, even though no energy release is likely from protein except in conditions of starvation, increased daily ingestion of protein by the athlete is suggested in order to supply the necessary building blocks for repair of muscle tissue. It may be interesting to note here that the dietary protein for highly successful eastern European athletes provides from 14 to 16 percent of total calories (54), a value roughly double that assigned by a "balanced diet."

So, on a day-to-day basis, we see the athlete on a high carbohydrate, high protein, low fat diet, with sufficient calories to maintain weight. This must not be mistaken for a reducing diet. In the average individual such a diet will surely lead to weight gain. The training athlete can easily determine whether or not his caloric intake is appropriate by daily weighing. A weight loss or gain would suggest an alteration in amounts consumed. Furthermore, one truly involved in heavy training would, we feel, be well-advised to supplement his diet daily with 500 milligrams of vitamin C, 400 international units of vitamin E and approximately 200 milligrams of iron in the form of ferrous sulfate with the following rationale: vitamin C is known to be involved with formation of new connective tissue, including capillary walls (51); vitamin E appears to be important relative to strength and structure of the skeletal muscle tissue (90); iron is an important component of hemoglobin (51). Perhaps supplementing the diet in this fashion is unnecessary for the athlete who does indeed avail himself of a truly balanced diet and maybe, as the Swedes say, the world's richest source of vitamins is urine from an American sport star! However, even though there is not a lot of evidence to support the concept that those in training require more than minimal daily requirements of vitamins and minerals, there isn't much contrary evidence, either. And those of us who have trained for competition know that the time and energy investment is so great that to take a chance on not realizing one's full potential is hardly worth a gamble when the likely loss is a few pennies a day. Furthermore, overdosing is unlikely since vitamin C is water soluble allowing excesses to be passed in the urine and vitamin E and iron have often been safely given in dosages several times greater than recommended.

The matter of meal placement has often been discussed. At one time we were all cautioned not to eat immediately prior to physical exertion, particularly not close to swimming. There was a fear that blood would be shunted away from the muscular walls of the stomach (the organ of digestion — not the abdomen) causing it to work in the relative absence of oxygen. This condition of ischemia theoretically would lead to cramps of the stomach, causing an irreversible doubling-up of the body. If in water, the tucked body would sink to the bottom which is a lot like drowning. Today we know the stomach will cease its work when skeletal muscles demand more blood. Even if one did suffer cramps of the muscular walls of the stomach, changes in posture would not ensue since those muscles are not attached to the skeleton. One may safely eat and immediately participate in recreational-type swimming.

In spite of the foregoing, neither the jogger nor the serious competitor should eat large meals closer than three hours before activity. When the stomach is full, it may interfere with movement of the diaphragm, the muscle which is responsible for sixty percent of the air exchanged at the lungs. Also, if the activity is to be prolonged, food in the stomach may ferment, producing substances which create nausea. We suggest that the pre-effort meal be at least three hours prior to actual initiation of that effort, and that it be very nearly fat-free but high in carbohydrate.

In 1967, Swedish researchers discovered that muscle glycogen stores could be significantly increased and work time prolonged by first training hard with little dietary carbohydrate and later resting with excess carbohydrate ingestion (13,62). This finding lead to the practice by athletes of "carbohydrate loading." There is reason to believe that this technique is effective, particularly if the impending effort shall be thirty minutes or more in duration, or if many repeated shorter efforts will be required over a period of time. Since one molecule of water is required for storing each molecule of muscle glycogen, weight gain must be expected when carbohydrate loading. Some argue that this extra water is a handicap to the athlete; others suggest it represents a water reservoir useful when perspiring heavily. Recently it has been shown that the amount of caffeine in a cup of coffee will result in mobilization of free fatty acids, a very important energy source for endurance performers, and that, therefore, the athlete may do well to drink coffee before his effort (29). This latter practice has not yet passed the test of time, but carbohydrate loading has. We suggest that the jogger who also competes in endurance racing carbohydrate load for an important event by training hard for five days while on a high-fat, low-carbohydrate diet, terminating this period with a long run three days before competition to deplete muscle glycogen stores. The three pre-race days should be days of rest and with free access to carbohydrate. Training should consist of light stretching and very short runs to barely reach a warm-up state. Extra sleep is important. At this time, supplementing the diet with vitamin C, vitamin E and iron seems especially appropriate. The day before competition should be devoid of running. We believe that tapering and carbohydrate loading should not be done more frequently than each six months, since the last thing we have here is a balanced diet!

Of course, when one works he perspires and the water and minerals lost in perspiration must be replaced. The best schedule for water replacement from a purely physiological standpoint is demand; i.e., drink when thirsty. This may not be practical. An adequate and practical schedule is to replace fluid every two miles while jogging, or every twenty minutes. Under race conditions this process is often possible, but it may not be so under conditions of casual jogging. Especially in the heat, the jogger must be very careful to avoid dehydration. If temperatures are extremely high a two-mile loop, beginning and terminating at a convenient watering place, should be arranged and used (21). The authors fully subscribe to the principles adopted by the American College of Sports Medicine (6) in regard to exercise in the heat.

Replacing minerals is a more technically difficult matter. Excess minerals taken in may remain in the body while throwing off the balance of water within body compartments. Over-doing rehydration, on the other hand, results only in more frequent visits to the bathroom. It has been reported that certain minerals actually increase in concentration in the body fluids during exercise since far more water is lost than are minerals (21). Taking salt tablets is not recommended. Generally, the taste for salt increases when bodily stores are depleted. Most people will recover lost sodium simply by using more table salt (sodium chloride) on foods. However, potassium, an important regulator of normal function, is not found in table salt. It must be replaced separately. Although tap water can be used to replace lost body water and sodium replaced by use of table salt, potassium must be brought in independently. Perhaps the simplest way to achieve this is to use one of the commercial athletic fluid replacement drinks, but water, table salt and a potassium tablet can be just as effective (21).

We do believe that someone has suggested beer as a replacement fluid. After thorough testing we can report that it *does* taste good, especially when the runner is hot and beer is chilled. Also, there are some rather pleasant side-effects. Sad to say, at least one respected authority (54) thinks that alcohol consumption may adversely affect the function of the liver, an organ so important in supplying energy substrates in exercise.

Generally, the endurance-trained athlete can fairly safely eat what he wants in quantities appropriate to desired weight maintenance, provided his fat intake is low and the vitamin and mineral intake is adequate. Carbohydrate loading twice a year may improve his performance in the "big ones." Fluid replacement as close to demand as possible is best, and steps to replace lost sodium and particularly potassium must be taken.

62

SUGGESTED READING

Bogert, L. J., Briggs, G. M. and Calloway, D. H., *Nutrition and Physical Fitness* (9th ed.). Philadelphia: W. B. Saunders, Co., 1973. Pp. xiii + 614.

Jokl, E. *Nutrition, Exercise and Body Composition.* Springfield, Ill.: Charles C. Thomas, Co., 1964. Pp. vii + 115.

Paish, W., *Diet in Sport.* West Yorkshire, Great Britain: E. P. Publishing, Limited, 1979. Pp. 93.

Williams, M. H., *Nutritional Aspects of Human Physical and Athletic Performance.* Springfield, Ill.: Charles C. Thomas, Co., 1976. Pp. xii + 444.

Young, D. R., *Physical Performance, Fitness and Diet.* Springfield, Ill.: Charles C. Thomas, Co., 1977. Pp. 113.

63

Chapter Twelve

Shoes, Shorts and Sweatsuits

The only things one really needs to jog are motivation and a good pair of shoes. Choice of shoes does represent a problem, however, and other articles of clothing can serve points of style and economics.

Shoes for jogging or running should be designed specifically for those activities and for no other purpose. The same can be said about footwear for other activities. Tennis shoes are made for playing tennis. They allow for lateral movements made frequently during the match. If used for jogging, they provide inadequate resistance to lateral slipping of the foot. Furthermore, tennis shoes have a low heel since the game of tennis is played from a platform formed by the balls of the feet. The heel rarely drops down forcefully to court level. On the other hand, quality jogging shoes have thick, well padded heels, since when jogging or running slowly, the heel strikes the running surface first. Running in tennis shoes allows the heel to drop too far, stretching the Achilles tendon, subsequently producing tendonitis.

Flexibility of the shoe sole is quite important. An unbending sole requires that the entire shoe be raised from the running surface simultaneously rather than piece-meal, a most inefficient movement. When examining new shoes, flexibility can be roughly determined by holding the heel firmly in one hand and bending the toe upward. The shoe should flex readily and the bend in the sole must be at a logical place; i.e., where the ball of the foot would be, instead of, for instance, at the arch.

There was a time when choosing a jogging shoe was simple, since only one company (Adidas) was producing them in quantity. These days, matters have become complicated. Not only are there Adidas shoes, but Nike, Tiger, Puma, Brooks, New Blance, Pony, Converse and probably a few others, left out by faulty memory. This list does not include the pseudo-training shoes sold by the mass-outlet stores. What, then, should one look for in a quality jogging shoe?

Heel stability is important. Does the shoe firmly grasp the heel and prevent lateral movement? When jogging, the direction of movement is straight ahead. there is a need to prevent side-to-side movements — they result in heel blisters, swollen ankles, tender spots on the knee and possibly even hip problems. In addition to firm grasp, the sole of the heel should provide stability through flared design, or by being wider than the heel cup as shown (exaggerated) below. The flared heel protects against twisting actions that can result when running on uneven surfaces such as grass, or when one steps on a stone, acorn or similar object.

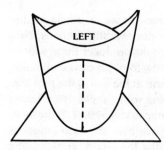 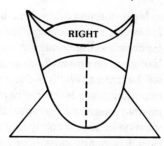

The soles of jogging shoes are designed for different purposes. A very rough, "nubby" sole is intended for use on a soft surface, like grass or earth. If used on asphalt or concrete these soles will wear out rapidly. Corrugated, rippled or grooved soles are for use on hard surfaces. If used on grass or earth they do not wear rapidly but sometimes fail to provide necessary traction. If the jogger is not certain which type of running surface will predominate in his training, or if he uses mixed surfaces, the smoother sole is recommended. Generally, the rubber-like material comprising the shoe sole will provide adequate traction except when racing.

Proper fit is critical to good shoe performance. For this reason we suggest that jogging shoes be purchased in a specialty shop where clerks have day-to-day practice in fitting the runner. The small town sporting goods shop may sell two or three pairs of running shoes weekly and fit them to the purchaser much as tennis or golf shoes are fitted. The outcome is bound to be dissatisfaction.

The jogging shoe should be somewhat longer than other

shoes, often a half- or even full-size larger than the street shoe. When standing in the running shoes, a thumb's width should separate the toe from the front tip of the shoe. This allows for some slight forward and backward shift of the foot without permitting the shoe upper from slightly lifting the large toenail at each stride. If the toenail is lifted each step, mile after mile, it will turn black and ultimately drop off. This dreaded jogger's ailment, although something of a status symbol, is not necessary.

Related to proper shoe length is the arch support. If the support fails to strike the arch of the foot properly and is uncomfortable the shoe may be too long or too short. The shoe must have a firm arch support, and it must not rub or otherwise irritate the foot.

Most training shoe manufacturers make a single width. However, several companies do produce width selections. New Balance has the greatest choice. Brooks produces three widths. If one has an unusually wide or narrow foot, his choice of makes will be limited. Width at the instep and at the ball of the foot is as important as it is at the heel. Also, some shoes have rather pointed toes and may crowd the foot causing blisters. If the laces must be pulled so tightly that the space over the shoe tongue is closed or nearly closed, or so that the toe box is wrinkled, the shoe is too wide. Don't count on the shoes to stretch if they feel a bit too narrow; one may have crippling blisters before they expand. Width fit is really best judged by the criteria of comfort. In this regard, remember to try on both shoes before purchase. Just because the left shoe fits doesn't necessarily mean the right one will.

Sometimes shoes will have all the desired features, but quality of workmanship is absent. Check to see that stitching is small, even and not too close to free edges. Be sure that soles are evenly and firmly affixed. Stand the shoes side-by-side on a table and at eye-level examine them from the rear. Are the heel cups

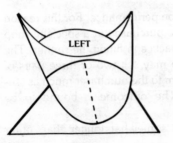
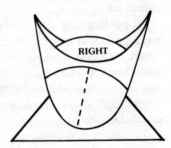

upright or are they canted as shown below? Is the sole of the heel of equal thickness on both sides of the heel? Canted heel cups or heels that are thicker on the outer as opposed to the inner surface (or vice versa) can create severe ankle, knee and hip damage.

Training shoes are expensive. Expect to pay from 30 to 60 dollars for them. If quality of workmanship or quality control are missing, don't buy them. If you do, you are not much better off than you'd be in pseudo-trainers or in tennis shoes.

Joggers are sometimes inclined to purchase the lightest shoe they can find. A quality jogging shoe will be lighter than an imitation or inexpensive one. However, do not purchase a racing shoe for training purposes even though it is lighter. Racing shoes are intended for occasional use — not for miles of training over rough terrain or hard surfaces. Furthermore, they do not provide sufficient cushioning effect or adequate support for daily runs.

When the jogger buys a quality pair of shoes that fit him properly he has invested a fairly large amount of money. It is money well spent. Such shoes are designed for the serious runner who may train 100 miles weekly or more. Although they may not last the true athlete more than three months, the jogger will own them for a year or more. And, with proper care, the already long life expectancy of the shoes can be extended. They should be washed whenever the need arises — they are constructed so that they might be. Jogging or racing shoes should not be dried in a clothes drier, though. Hang them up in the sun or in an air-conditioned room.

Become acquainted with *Shoe-Goo,*® or similar products. These rapid-drying glues can be used to reinforce worn spots on the soles, particularly at the heels. It is normal for the heels to wear on the outside, but should the wear penetrate to the spongy middle sole, the life of the shoe is very limited from that event onward. When the outer sole becomes thin, a layer of *Shoe-Goo* will prevent damage and shoe life can be doubled — perhaps tripled in the case of the jogger — by this simple expedient. One caution — do not build up the heel thickness so that it tilts the heel. Such unevenness precipitates injury.

How about ladies' shoes? Some ladies shoes fit ladies — or men — better than do the male varieties. If you are looking for a narrow size, ladies' models may be especially appropriate.

What happens if the shoes show signs of faulty manufacture or fit after several wearings? Take them back. If the merchant is reluctant to accept them, remind him that joggers are dedicated, long-lived and inclined to purchase many pairs of shoes in their lifetime. He'll take them back!

Shorts are largely a matter of style. Actually, one can jog in anything that provides reasonable freedom of movement. But shorts made especially for jogging or running *are* rather "statusy." If one plans to spring for real running shorts, buy more than just a name. Look for shorts with smooth, overcast seams to prevent chafing. Women should closely examine the ladies' models since they are tailored to accommodate the slightly broader female pelvis. Make certain the shorts are made of the light-weight, easy-to-dry materials. A most sensible characteristic of jogging shorts is the ability to go into the post-run shower and come out clean and readily driable. Men should consider shorts with built-in nylon web supporters. Although there is little risk that running without support will jiggle things out of functional perspective, a smooth, light supporter does prevent chafing. In passing, allow us to mention that if chafing of groin or thighs is a problem, consider *Vaseline*® as an answer.

Any kind of T-shirt or tank shirt is just fine for jogging. Shirts are rather difficult to wring out by hand, so taking them to the shower is not too practical. Therefore, they should be made of readily washable materials that can also be dried outdoors or in an automatic drier. Frequently specially designed shirts are provided to the top finishers in road races. Wearing these, rightfully won, "can't be beat" for function and prestige while jogging.

Sweatsuits are intended for cold weather. They should not be worn, nor should plastic or rubber suits, for purposes of weight loss while exercising. Weight shed by excessive perspiration is regained in short order and in fact is utterly meaningless. The type of sweatsuit worn in cold weather, then, becomes, once more, a matter of choice and style. One can quite easily spend some 75 to 125 dollars on a sweatsuit that serves no greater function than a set of "baggies" purchased at a discount store. Keep in mind when shopping that once running, the environment is seldom as cold as it first appeared, and that articles discarded on the initial lap are often not visible on subsequent ones. The best sweatsuit is one that preserves body heat and permits freedom of movement. It should be used from the beginning when climate demands, or following a run on a cool day. Otherwise, it serves no useful purpose.

Really, in the final analysis, what one wears is a matter of personal choice, except for shoes. As long as the foundation is firm and its stability preserved, the bodily remainder can be shrouded

in whatever seems necessary to the individual — except that
rules of propriety and law need be followed!

SUGGESTED READING

Fixx, James F., *The Complete Book of Running.* New York: Random House,
1977. Pp. xxii + 314.

Running Review Staff, Running shoe construction. *Running Review,* 2:12-19,
1978.

Schuster, R. O., Running footwear. *Running Review,* 2:56-57, 1978.

Chapter Thirteen

Jogging in the Heat or Cold

Most joggers have a vision that comes to mind readily in which they see themselves running free in shorts and singlet, cool breeze whipping the hair, spring flowers and green grass evident everywhere. A pleasant situation, surely, but really a rather uncommon one. Most joggers spend many days plodding in heat and humidity, sweat flooding from every pore, and just as many more bundled against numbing cold. Maybe pleasant days are well remembered because they are unusual!

Exercising on a cool, dry day is pleasant because there is a single stressor — the exercise. Stress is doubled, in a sense, by severe weather. Obviously then, restraint is indicated on "bad days." Either the pace or the duration, or both, must be modified. However, we are not suggesting that the daily run be cancelled, except on the most inclement of days. Perhaps the jogger most dangerous to himself is the intermittent one. Dropping out because of bad weather leads to work-outs separated by too much time with super-strenuous efforts made afterwards in an attempt to regain lost ground. Injuries commonly result. So, run we must, even on rather poor days. Actually, the climate is rarely as bad as it appears at first glance and the good feelings that always come with jogging ultimately appear, although perhaps a little delayed.

Hot days, particularly if they are humid, represent the greatest threat to the jogger. Exercise increases the metabolic rate since more energy is required than while at rest. Heat production accompanies energy release. On a hot day, not only does the body need to contend with the heat it produces, but also with the high environmental temperature. Heat transfer is accomplished by conduction (direct contact with a cooler substance), convection (carriage by air currents) and evaporation (of perspiration from the body surface). On a hot day conduction becomes inefficient since ambient temperature may approach body temperature. Convection retains some utility since the moving body passes briskly through air. Evaporation of perspiration loses effectiveness since the body becomes drenched. Dripping perspiration is a poor way to dissipate heat. A thin film of water much more rapidly evaporates and cools. Furthermore, if it is humid, evaporation rate is inhibited since the nearly saturated air has little space for additional water molecules. The outcome of all this is that at least two of the three ways the body has to rid itself of heat lose efficiency. At the very best, body temperature soars and fatigue intervenes. However, there are other potential outcomes. One can perspire so profusely that dehydration is threatened. The body may respond by closing down the sweat mechanism. The skin becomes hot and dry, body temperature climbs and heat stroke can occur. Heat stroke, even when properly treated, can be damaging to the central nervous system and even fatal.

Exercising for a number of days in the heat may gradually produce water and mineral imbalances which can be very nearly as dangerous as acute heat stroke. As described in Chapter Ten, water and mineral substances lost in perspiration must be replaced.

Well, it seems to be one of those ". . . damned if you do, damned if you don't" situations. Omitting many days of jogging because of heat seems ill-advised, and jogging on those scorchers can be outright dangerous. What is to be done? Some suggestions follow.

Unless you are well acclimatized (one year or more of exposure to either tropic or sub-tropic conditions) *do not* jog when the environmental temperature exceeds 90°F *(32°C)*. We hasten to point out that even in Florida it is rarely that warm between 9:00 P.M. and 9:00 A.M.

When it is hotter than usual, slow the pace and shorten the distance. It has been suggested (21) that when jogging in the heat one should not cover more than two miles or go for longer than 20 minutes without replenishing water lost in perspiration. It is a fairly simple matter, and a procedure which may save a life, to lay out a two-mile "hot day loop" beginning and ending at the front door. This arrangement allows for a drinking stop at appropriate intervals, and also permits long work-outs by repetition of the loop.

If it is a genuine scorcher, stay out of the sun. This is best accomplished by running at night or in the early morning. If that alternative is impossible, seek a shady route, wear a white hat that will shade the nose and ears, put a sunscreen lip balm not

71

only on the lips, but on the nose as well, and wear a shirt. The shirt will protect against sunburn, but also hold perspiration, allowing it to evaporate slowly, thus producing an excellent cooling effect.

Even though heat stress maladies often strike the jogger with no warning, try to listen to your body. If extremely weary, burning hot, light-headed, nauseous or suffering loss of peripheral vision, *stop*. Walk home slowly. Try again another day when conditions are better. After all, health and life are much more important than whatever amount of pride is damaged by inability to finish the task.

If a persistent heat wave is your lot, remember to replenish lost water after each work-out. Potassium depletion is a real threat under these conditions, so be sure to consume foodstuffs high in that element (bananas, oranges). And consider every-other-day runs for the duration of the bad weather.

How about running in a summer rain? Delightful, cooling and refreshing! But a caution or two: don't be the highest thing on the horizon if there is lightning, and be aware that shoes made heavy by water certainly generate ballistic forces that can create muscle and joint injury. In other words, when you see that ominous flash in the sky get indoors, in a car, in a forest of many trees or into a ditch. And, take a shorter stride when your shoes are soggy.

Cold weather produces a different set of circumstances, but unless really extreme, winter conditions have less severe implications than does summer heat. As with heat, cold is a relative thing, its severity vastly dependent upon human interpretation. The present writer has run in Sweden in February and March. As a permanent Florida resident, the cold was excruciating, penetrating sweatsuit and long underwear with ease. To make matters worse, my heat-acclimatized body responded as it always does during a run by pouring out huge quantities of perspiration. Layers of clothing, including the woolen cap, rapidly became saturated. Icicles were my constant companion, and the last half of the run was as comfortable as it would have been had I pre-soaked my clothes and then attempted a few miles at sub-freezing temperatures. Meanwhile, my Swedish colleagues, jogging in the same city park, appeared just a bit rosy and quite comfortable in shorts and light sweat shirt! Indeed, I am aware that my suffering was so evident as to create concern in adult strollers and fear in the hearts of children.

In the midst of winter, continue to exercise your body while

72

also exercising some good judgment. A sweatsuit is an excellent investment. By the way, a cheap pair of baggies is every bit as protective as expensive, well-fitting jacket and pants suits. A hat to cover the ears is a must since one way in which your body conserves heat is to restrict circulation to the extremities. Little blood in the ears, nose, fingers and toes predispose them to freezing or frostbite. Gloves are important. If you perspire profusely, get gloves that can be washed. Some joggers prefer the no-socks feeling, but in the winter, socks are required. Rather thick cotton is best, but be sure to not have them so thick that the shoes no longer fit properly. Don't make the mistake of omitting shorts under the sweat pants, and men should furthermore wear a supporter. All sorts of projections can become frostbitten and there have actually been cases of severely cold-affected genitals in male joggers. No fooling!

Winter in many climes brings snow and ice. More often than not, areas used for jogging are cleared of such hazards; but for one reason or another, sometimes they are not. Of course, ice and hard-packed snow are dangerous because they are slippery. If the route is completely covered by packed snow or ice, find another place. Should the path be largely cleared but with slippery patches, walk over the slippery stuff. If, in spite of all precautions, you should slip while jogging try to let yourself fall. The bumps and bruises received by body and dignity will be far less debilitating than the stretched tendon, ligament or muscle one might acquire in the process of scrambling to prevent a tumble. Unfortunately, the reflex is to catch oneself and most of us have neither presence of mind nor the kind of control required to just relax upon losing footing, and go down.

Deep snow poses unique disadvantages. It absorbs heat from feet and legs. In addition, it greatly alters jogging style, creating mechanical inefficiency. It is, in the latter respect, a bit like running in soft sand. Runs in deep snow should be much shorter than those enjoyed under usual conditions in order to prevent cold injury to feet and legs and to avoid exhaustion.

In the cold, as in the heat, it is best to structure a special jogging loop that brings one back to warmth and shelter at rather frequent intervals, say every two miles, or each 20 minutes. In temperate climates where both severe heat and cold are standard, the same loop can easily be used for both conditions.

Every winter, newspapers report people found unconscious or dead in the cold, having fallen on ice or packed snow, or having exhausted themselves in deep snow. If you discovered someone unconscious, obviously suffering from exposure, what should be done? Get him to warm shelter, first of all. Do not attempt the rub with snow routine, Jack London notwithstanding. Warm the torso and abdomen. Expose the limbs only to the warmth of the indoor air that now surrounds them. Do not massage or chafe the limbs. To do so will return the chilled blood in these extremities to the central circulation, further reducing the temperature of the blood servicing vital organs. If the temperature in the thorax (chest) goes no lower than 80 °F (27 °C) survival is possible. Blood in the arms and legs of our victim may be as low as 60 °F (16 °C).

There are some dangers associated with jogging in extreme weather, but there are some rewards as well. The cool drink after a hot run tastes like no other. The visual and tactile beauty of a summer shower is unknown to those who have never run through one. Designs formed of icy tree limbs and black patterns against a snowy background are not well seen from an automobile window, nor are these beauties viewed in any safer manner than from afoot. And as with all things, when one knows of the risks, he is armed against them. Instead of an excuse, a "bad day" may actually become an incentive, since it is an opportunity for an unusual and challenging experience.

SUGGESTED READING

American College of Sports Medicine, *Physiological Aspects of Sports and Physical Fitness*. Chicago: Athletic Institute, 1968. Pp. 102.

Burke, E. J. (ed.), *Toward an Understanding of Human Performance*. Ithaca, NY: Mouvement Publications, 1977. Pp. iv + 92.

Drinkwater, B. L., Kuprat, I. G., Denton, J. E. and Horvath, S. M., Heat tolerance of female distance runners. *Annals of the New York Academy of Sciences*, 301:777-792, 1977.

Straus, R. H. (ed.), *Sports Medicine and Physiology*. Philadelphia: W. B. Saunders Company, 1979. Pp. xi + 441.

Chapter Fourteen

What To Do With Your Head While Jogging

Man is a thinking animal. About 99 percent of the time, that is good. But sometimes we humans think ourselves into predicaments, or out of successes. Actually, what one is, is fairly well an outcome of what he always thought he was. To substantiate that concept, we offer the observation that every language has no shortage of phrases such as ". . . just as I thought . . .," ". . . I told you so . . .," ". . . they always said . . .," and ". . . I knew it all along . . .". Sometimes people never attempt something (or anything!) because they are sure they know the outcome. On the other hand, some folks try the strangest things — for the same reason! Would one cross above Niagara Falls on a tight wire if he weren't certain he'd make it? We are likely to consider the latter sort of individual as just plain audacious, but really, he is not any more apprehensive about what he does than are we about what we do. Each of us merely "knows" the outcomes of his endeavors.

We have an acquaintance — a young man — who keeps company with an older woman who treats him badly. His self-image is so poor that he is certain he can do no better. Furthermore, he will not shop for fear of losing what he has. And, don't we all know people who truly *need* jogging but who won't begin because they somehow, magically, just *know* they can't do that sort of thing.

Everyone has such "thinking problems," including the active jogger. How often have we heard the initiate exclaim, "I'll celebrate when I can jog a mile!"" From his vantage point, and knowing what he does about himself, a mile seems like the ultimate accomplishment. Don't tell him he may one day not feel adequately warmed-up after a mile, or that there are people much like himself who routinely run ten-mile road races. These things, he "knows" are not possible for him. Even those who have been running for years typically have certain theories about themselves which limit their performances.

Just about everyone who jogs strives to improve by attempting more challenging distances or paces. Usually improvements are gradually achieved, and this slow approach is safest. Our attempt in this chapter is not to provide a means to produce immediate and spectacular performance increments, but rather to reveal a method to "get the head out of the way" of working toward goals already within reach.

Very often, an improved time over a well-known jogging route occurs spontaneously and without a conscious effort. It isn't uncommon for this phenomenon to happen some time after the runner had given up on attempts to achieve just such an effect. He has, in fact, disassociated from the chore — and accomplished it! Once thinking about all the factors (hills, weariness, heat, cold, pain, nausea) that might interfere with his effort had ceased, he became less conscious of them and secured the goal. This runner was, in fact, capable of running the desired time all along — but his head had been getting in the way.

Dissasociation provides a means to achieve jogging goals, and there are many ways to disassociate. Most simply, one can merely think about something other than jogging and its appended sensations. We don't know of anyone who does not sometimes disassociate in this fashion, even though most joggers haven't really thought about it in this context. The "other thoughts" range from professional considerations through family matters to sexual fantasies (so we are told). It is probably close akin to simple day-dreaming, but done while jogging or running. There have been tales told of architects planning buildings room-by-room as they exercise, of physicians who perfect complicated surgical procedures, and of lawyers who structure a strong defense while running mile after mile. An interesting and revealing game can be played at parties by having those in attendance relate their favorite jogging fantasies. It is amazing how many can project themselves into heroic or philanthropic roles of vast magnitude while ambulating along at what is indeed a pedestrian pace in the truest sense of the term! And then there are parents who imagine their children smashing world records and winning Rhodes scholarships. Always there is the sweet young thing who can only blush when asked, and avert her eyes. Whatever they think, one and all — they are disassociating.

One can disassociate simply be being intensely aware of his

surroundings — seeing birds and plants, feeling breezes, noting figures in the clouds. This may really be the most common of all ways to separate one's self from his jogging. One gentleman of our acquaintance has taught himself to self-hypnotize but prefers to avoid that practice since it eliminates intense involvement with natural surroundings.

What about hypnosis? Can it help? Is it a form of disassociation? Hypnosis is a very effective way to disassociate and it can remove obstacles to running performance. Some professional athletes have relied heavily upon hypnosis to improve their play. It must be understood that use of hypnotism cannot produce sudden, superhuman efforts, however. Rather, it is best applied in reducing obstructions to hard and productive practice, or to increase confidence in ability.

An amateur hypnotist can be dangerous. Many psychiatrists are trained in hypnotism. They are also expensive. With a little effort, mostly in the form of reading, one can learn the scientific underpinnings of hypnotism (65) and learn to self-hypnotize (91). Danger and expense are relatively minor factors when one self-hypnotizes, and the skill, once well-developed, may become the most valuable tool in the user's repertoire, not only as it concerns jogging, but in relation to other aspects of his life, too.

A prerequisite to successful self-hypnotism is a state of relaxation. To achieve this, lie supine on a comfortable bed in a familiar room, legs fully extended with arms at the sides. Let the eyes close. Think only about relaxing. Concentrate first on fully relaxing the face, particularly the powerful jaw muscles. Relax the muscles of the neck and shoulders, then of the upper arms and upper back. Eliminate all muscle tension in the forearms, hands, chest and abdomen. Relax the muscles of lower back, legs and feet. Tell yourself you are so fully relaxed that there is no muscle pressure on blood vessels. The heart and breathing rates are perfect for this task — easy, relaxed, efficient. Now count backward from 50 to zero, slowly and in a measured, methodical cadence. If drowsiness interferes, return to the last number clearly recalled as counted and begin again from there. You may fall asleep — no problem. Always resume the count and continue until zero is reached. Make this a nightly ritual. It will aid sleep and set a reasonable time span for the next step in learning to self-hypnotize.

A convenient and efficient approach to self-hypnosis is the Five Breath Method (91). After practicing relaxation and the countdown described above for a week or ten days, alter the procedure by keeping the eyes open and eliminating the countdown. Otherwise, relax in the usual manner. When fully relaxed, visually focus on an object over the head, such as the ceiling lamp. Take a normal breath, silently count it as one, and exhale. Repeat this three more times, noting each breath by number. The eyes remain open and focused. The fifth breath is a large one — as deep a breath as is comfortable. Name it "five," and hold it while counting backward from five to zero. As zero is pronounced, exhale and close the eyes. Practice the process each evening until it creates a light sleep followed by a brief but clear period of wakefulness, followed by sleep through the night.

The next step is to produce post-hypnotic suggestions. These are merely promptings for action in the future after the period of self-hypnosis. Post-hypnotic suggestions must always be couched in positive terms. Never suggest what will not be, but rather what *will* be. We recommend that the first suggestion be this:

"When I awake I shall be completely rested and relaxed." Print those words in large capital letters on a 3 x 5 index card. Prior to inducing self-hypnosis, read the words carefully to yourself ten times, being sure to see each word clearly. Then apply the Five Breath Method.

Of course, what one suggests is a personal matter. It is possible to precipitate self-improvement in many areas such as study habits, reading speed, memory, personal habits — and jogging proficiency. One post-hypnotic suggestion that all practitioners of self-hypnosis should apply is:

"I will have confidence in myself as a hypnotist." Joggers might consider the following suggestions:

"Pain from fatigue is minor"

"I am ready for a faster pace"

"I am ready for 3 (5, 7, 10) miles"

"I can train daily"

"My heart (lungs, legs) is (are) strong and durable"

"I am a talented runner."

Every jogger has a problem he'd like to overcome and self-hypnosis can gradually aid him to do so. Therefore, post-hypnotic suggestions of the most precise nature are best self-formulated.

It is possible to self-hypnotize while jogging. As a matter of fact, the rhythmic nature of the activity is a great stimulus to achieving an hypnotic state. This practice, indulged in by the inexperienced, can have some unwanted outcomes. Directions to the subconscious mind must always explicitly permit awareness of threatening aspects of the environment, including traffic, dogs, other people, obstacles in the path and maintenance of desired route. Self-hypnotizing while jogging is best practiced after considerable experience with the Five Breath Method in the security of the home. Never direct that there will be no pain. A lovely batch of blisters, or something worse, may well be the result.

To hypnotize while jogging repeat the phrase "Drowsier and drowsier" again and again in cadence to your foot-falls. Continue until in fact you do seem drowsy. Now, again in cadence with the pace repeat 20 times, counting on the fingers. "The subconscious mind will regulate the pace." It is important to employ such a phrase since self-hypnosis while jogging is perhaps the most powerful means of disassociation. Somebody must be left in charge for the untended machine may overdo. The individual can devise suggestions to use from this point on, composing them with special interests in mind. Suggestions are best repeated 20 times, always in cadence with the pace. When the legs grow tight, "Relax, relax," may prove useful. "Breathing easy," frequently seems appropriate. Each practitioner will eventually discover phrases to repeat that have special personal meaning. These seem to function best if kept as an unshared item.

It becomes especially difficult to disassociate if one practices some habit that constantly zeros in on present conditions. Regulating length of stride is such a practice. Carrying a watch while jogging fits well in this category also. We are all interested in speed. If one must know his elapsed time he should call the local time-of-day service as he starts his run and again immediately upon completing it. The resulting time lacks precision, but exact mile-to-mile times can be depressing and exhausting.

Disassociation may be helpful in the jogging or practice situation. It can be a disaster during competition. Even in the course of a marathon the racer must keep his goals clearly in his conscious mind. Concentration on pace, strategy, distance covered and distance remaining is a must. We emphasize that disassociation if a tool best utilized to remove obstacles that obstruct gradual application of greater stress in *practice* runs. In no way do we mean to suggest that hypnotism or any other form of disassociation can favorably affect competitive performance except as it allows for better preparation through more effective practice.

For the average jogger who runs for fun and for better health, intense disassociation is unnecessary. His usual patterns of daydreaming or of observing nature will suffice. However, the skill is worth developing nevertheless, since it has many applications and yet could also help the weary runner complete the last mile at optimal pace with minimal stress and discomfort.

SUGGESTED READING

Fromm, E. and Shor, R. E., *Hypnosis*. Chicago: Aldine-Atherton, Inc., 1972. Pp. xiv + 656.

Hilgard, J. R., *Personality and Hypnosis*. Chicago: The University of Chicago Press, 1970. Pp. x + 304.

LeCron, L. M., *Self Hypnotism*. New York: The New American Library, Inc., 1970. Pp. 208.

Straub, W. F. (ed.), *Sport Psychology*, (2nd ed.), Ithaca, N.Y.: Mouvement Publications, 1980. Pp. iv + 295.

Wolberg, L. R., *Hypnosis — Is It For You?* New York: Harcourt Brace Jovanovich, Inc., 1972. Pp. xviii + 299.

Chapter Fifteen

Mechanics of Jogging, and Other Nuts and Bolts

A common fallacy has it that walking, jogging and running are activities so natural to Man that no one has to be taught to do them. If any teaching were required, it was done by those finest of all teachers and people, parents. Now, we all know that most parents aren't great teachers, particularly not of their own children. Otherwise, we'd have a reduced need for psychiatrists in this society. And, if one is inclined to believe that everyone walks properly, he should stop and watch a few stroll by. The variety of gaits and postures is amazing. They can't all be right. Observing joggers is even more revealing. The idea that we all run well is counter-indicated by the fact that few of us can approach world records.

We do not advocate that everyone jog precisely the same way. There is room for individual differences. However, certain basic rules of mechanical action apply to all, or surely to nearly all.

It would be nice if at this point in the discussion jogging could be accurately and concisely defined. That is difficult to do. One cannot assign a pace, say eight minutes per mile, and claim anything faster is running. An eight-minute mile is running for some and jogging for others. One is tempted to say that jogging is a gait faster than walking in which the heel contacts the ground sooner than does the toe. But examination by film of four-minute milers shows their heels, too, frequently strike first. Are they jogging? The best we can do is suggest that if the pace is definitely faster than walking but the participant can still easily converse with companions, he is jogging, not running.

In spite of the problem with definition, mechanical characteristics of jogging can be identified. For instance, the heel does strike the ground before the toe. Many beginners, especially women, strive for an up-on-the-toes method, apparently for aesthetic reasons. Forget about gracefulness. Jogging is kind of plopping along. The ease with which it is done lends grace. Running on the toes soon becomes laborious and the grace is gone. Let the heel strike first, then roll the weight forward over the toes.

Take a short stride. It is an efficient means to transfer weight from one foot to the next. Although it is easy to imagine oneself loping along with a long stride much like an antelope, in fact the appearance is more giraffe-like. Furthermore, a long stride straightens the knee, reducing the shock-absorbing quality of that structure. Instead of being absorbed at the flexed knee, impact forces travel to the spine, frequently producing low back pain.

The posture is erect, although a slight forward lean when traveling uphill is acceptable. An erect position allows for observation down the trail so that hazards may be avoided. More important, rounding the shoulders and curling the upper spine restricts breathing movements. Also, the weight of the torso is most efficiently carried when balanced nearly directly over the center of gravity.

There is much individual variation regarding arm carriage. In a very general description, it can be said that arm position should be comfortable, elbows somewhat bent and swinging in a natural fashion. Natural arm swing implies that when stepping out with the right leg, the right arm shall counterbalance by moving backward, and vice versa. It is the rare individual who will reverse this process. Generally, it is accomplished without thought. The direction of arm swing should be forward and backward along the axis of travel. It is most inefficient mechanically to swing the arms across the body. The amount of elbow flexion is a matter of individual choice, the only guideline being that arm and shoulder muscles should feel rather relaxed most of the time. When one runs faster, arm swing becomes more vigorous. This is an outcome of the speedier pace and should not be consciously sought.

Breathing is another factor that is best just left alone. The rate and depth of breathing are controlled reflexly by carbon dioxide levels and acid-base balance in the blood, and by neural pathways with receptors in the skeletal muscle. The runner need not think about breathing deeper, "harder" or faster. That is all regulated for him. Some beginning joggers attempt to breathe only through the nose, usually again for aesthetic reasons, but sometimes because they've always heard that passing air through the nasal passages cleanses it. When jogging, the volume of air per unit of time required for adequate exposure to O_2 is so great that breathing must be done through both mouth and nose. One can look good and cleanse inspired air 23.5 hours daily. A half-hour of mouth breathing will destroy neither the image nor the lungs.

What about knock-knees, bowlegs, pigeon-toes and weak ankles? We have jogging friends with all these problems, although not with all of them at once. Of course, there are orthopedic problems that preclude jogging, but slow progress and willingness to regress in training when difficulties arise allow most to jog to some extent even if they are less than perfect from the waist down. If pain or swelling in the lower extremities occurs, check your shoes for manufacturing defects as described in Chapter Twelve. Also examine to be sure the heels are wearing on the outside borders. Have a friend observe to see if both feet are doing the same things, or if the ankles are dropping inward or outward. Whether or not sources are identified, plan to see a jogging orthopedist or podiatrist. Take the shoes to the appointment. Often devices can be fitted to prevent difficulties in the future. And, if jogging is a no-no, it is best to know it beforehand.

Two very common jogging ailments are shin splints and Achilles' tendonitis. Sometimes these arise from using a surface that is either too hard or too soft. A soft surface requires a forceful toe-push in order to propel away from the ground into the next stride. Pushing hard with the toes stretches the muscles of the front of the lower leg and can generate shin splints. Hard surfaces such as concrete or asphalt exaggerate the pounding of the heel, and the shock immediately is transmitted to the large tendon at the rear of the lower leg. The tendon can thus become inflamed and tender.

Muscle soreness is generally a major problem only when beginning a jogging program, and slow progress from walking to jogging can greatly reduce its incidence even then. Muscle soreness may return to the seasoned jogger after an effort at a faster pace. This is due to the fact that faster running necessitates a higher knee lift. Jogging requires very little knee lift and, therefore, the muscles that perform that action are relatively unconditioned.

Whenever there is soreness or swelling in muscles or joints due to exercise, apply cold, never heat. Cold will constrict capillaries and prevent fluid from leaking into the injured area to produce more swelling, pressure and pain. Heat application will do the reverse, dilating the capillaries and flooding the injured area. Unless your physician indicates otherwise, ice is always the answer.

If a tendonitis is suspected, cold applications every three or four hours are useful, as are ten grains of aspirin each four hours while awake, provided your doctor agrees. The aspirin is an excellent anti-inflammatory agent, and also reduces discomfort.

Ingrown great toenails are dangerous, besides being painful. Infection is a common complication. Once full-blown, self-treatment is ill-advised. A podiatrist is best equipped to deal with it and can take proper steps to avoid infection and stimulate rapid recovery. For prevention of ingrown toenails, routinely trim them rather short and file the center top of the nail so that it is thinner in the middle than on the sides. This will encourage the corners of the nail to lift rather than grow inward. Also, remember that the jogging shoe should be a bit longer than the street shoe.

All these ailments and advisements surely sound threatening, but every activity has its dangers. We knew a man who stayed home most of his life to avoid injury. One evening a coal truck lost its brakes coming down the old hill and smashed into our friend's house, killing him. If jogging is appealing and produces satisfactions, do it. At least it is self-regulating and, if problems ensue, one can stop and/or attempt remedies.

SUGGESTED READING

Broer, M. R. and Zernicke, R. F., *Efficiency of Human Movement* (4th ed.). Philadelphia: W. B. Saunders Company, 1979. Pp. xi + 427.

Cooper, J. M. and Glassow, R. B., *Kinesiology* (2nd ed.). St. Louis: The C. V. Mosby Co., 1968. Pp. x + 310.

Hay, J. G., *The Biomechanics of Sports Techniques* (2nd ed.). Englewood Cliffs, NJ: Prentice-Hall, Inc., 1978. Pp. xvii + 519.

Scriber, K. and Burke, E. J. (eds.). *Relevant Topics in Athletic Training*. Ithaca, NY: Mouvement Publications, 1978. Pp. iv + 140.

Simonian, C., *Fundamentals of Sports Biomechanics*. Englewood Cliffs, NJ: Prentice-Hall, Inc., 1981. Pp. xv + 221.

Chapter Sixteen

The Beauty-Function Parallel

If a thing has no function, it has no beauty. Furthermore, the greater the function, the greater the beauty. Each of us in his own way comes to recognize and accept these truths. Some seem to know them immediately and instinctively; others are destined to confront them time and again without understanding. But eventually there is always realization. Beauty and function are synonymous.

Things that are useful are beautiful. The longer they function, the more lovely they become. A tool that always gets the job done, that is smooth and polished from the user's hand, is far more beautiful than is a new but unproved duplicate in the showcase. The patina of age that lends a deep glow of beauty to antique furniture is there from years of use. The grace of the antique exceeds that of the new piece because of its proven function. An old friendship that has served both members well for years has a loveliness of function that cannot be approached by new acquaintances, no matter how promising the future. An old friendship has survived the stresses of interpersonal relationships and gains beauty through performance.

On the other hand, think of things usually considered ugly and generally they are found also to be without significant function. A dilapidated and abandoned house is an eyesore primarily because it is without its intended purpose. This is in contrast to such a structure as the ancient Roman coliseum at Arles, France, hundreds of years old, but still in daily use. Even the great Roman and Greek ruins retain their beauty since they continue to illustrate basic principles of architecture. There is a beautiful clock in the cathedral at Lund, Sweden. It is made of wood and arranged to ring the massive bells in the tower several times daily. Also at several times during the day two knights upon horses clash violently, all driven by the clockworks. This clock has functioned for hundreds of years. One would hardly purchase a similar item for the home, but this one is beautiful because it has served so well, and seems capable of continuing forever.

Almost everyone reaches a point of maturity that drives him to evaluate his life, a life that may have seemed beautiful, perhaps because of pleasant surroundings, material gains and professional advancements. Frequently, the reassessment instead reveals an ugly life without real function. This discovery sometimes leads to drastic alteration of lifestyle on the part of the involved individual. Often a frantic, belated effort is made to lend beauty to the life by means of great social contribution. The beauty-function parallel is recognized!

There really isn't anything that violates the principle: Where there is function, there is beauty. A thing ugly at first glance can prove beautiful upon observation of its function. People sometimes surround construction sites to gaze enraptured at the function of huge, earth-moving implements which are certainly homely while at rest. An auto mechanic is likely to describe a grease-covered engine as beautiful, and has, of course, its function in mind. A football fan can recall feats of great skill which he has observed and will refer to them as beautiful. Yet none of us can honestly describe the players who participate in this violent game as beautiful, at least not in the common sense of the word.

The human body abides by the principle that beauty follows function. We have grown to accept that a slim, strong, healthy body is beautiful. Things that interfere with body function are often seen as ugly. Human gracefulness is admired because it illustrates efficiency of movement. Unfortunately, handicaps that interfere with function traditionally have been regarded as ugly. Quasimoto was abhorred because of his limiting deformity. The blind have so often been considered unattractive, and their only deficiency is a lack of a function. Fortunately, today many people have learned to see beauty in quality of function within limits set by existing potential.

The epitome of human beauty is the performing dancer or athlete. These bodies are trained to produce their maximal function, and are in possession of greater skills than most can call upon. But any one of us can enhance personal beauty by expanding function. There are many ways to achieve this. Most of our social institutions are designed to aid in this endeavor. We can educate ourselves to allow for a full intellectual development, apply to religion to aid us in selecting good and useful acts, seek the law for social structure to properly channel our efforts and maintain our health through use of hospitals and similar institutions. Furthermore, we are obliged to stimulate full function of our bodies by application of sensible habits of diet, sleep and exercise. To ignore this requirement is to destroy the foundation upon which all other personal development is based. It is a senseless destruction of beauty through loss of function.

Of course, it is a matter of values. We cannot force our feelings and opinions upon others. To become missionary in our zeal succeeds only in driving off potential converts. Some claims made by exercise advocates are without substantiation and are, in fact, silly. Intelligent people will not buy the product when the advertising defies reason. An intense jogging advocate recently suggested, for instance, that running a few miles was a better experience for him than making love. Either we don't know how to jog, or *he* doesn't know how to make love.

But striving for the best bodily function within existing limitation is a good and useful thing to do. It is to some very nearly a religious act in that they see themselves carrying out a basic commandment from a Superior Being. We submit that time spent attending to bodily needs pleases God who surely gave us bodies to *use*. As the reader might judge, the days of guilty conscience regarding jogging when we could be doing "something else" are well behind us. We can wave and smile at those of other persuasions, for we, too, are attending to a portion of our daily devotion, as surely as are they! We shall don our ceremonial shorts and worship in our wordless way while joyfully maintaining the Temple of God.

SUGGESTED READING

Cannon, W. B., *The Wisdom of the Body*. New York: W. W. Norton and Co., Inc., 1939. Pp. xvii + 333.

Santayana, G., *The Sense of Beauty*. New York: Charles Scribner's Sons, 1902. Pp. ix + 275.

Selected References

1. Adams, W. C., Fox, R. H., Fry, A. J. and MacDonald, I. C., Thermoregulation during marathon running in cool, moderate and hot environments. *Journal of Applied Physiology*, 38:1030-1037, 1975.

2. Adams, W. C., McHenry, M. M. and Bernauer, C. M., Long-term physiologic adaptations to exercise with special reference to performance and cardiorespiratory function in health and disease. *The American Journal of Cardiology*, 33:765-775, 1974.

3. Adlersberg, David, Schaefer, Louis E., Steinberg, Arthur G. and Wang, C. I., Age, sex, serum lipids and coronary atherosclerosis. *Journal of American Medical Association*, 162:619-622, 1956.

4. Albright, T. E., Which sports for girls? In: Harris, D. V. (ed.), *DGWS Reports: Women in Sports:* Washington, D.C.: AAHPER, 1971.

5. Albrink, Margaret J. and Meigs, J. Wister, Interrelationships between skinfold thickness, serum lipids and blood sugar in normal men. *American Journal of Clinical Nutrition*, 15:255-261, 1964.

6. American College of Sports Medicine, *Physiological Aspects of Sports and Physical Fitness*. Chicago: Athletic Institute, 1968.

7. American College of Sports Medicine, Position statement on prevention of heat injuries during distance running. *Medicine and Science in Sports*, 7:vii-ix, 1975.

8. American Heart Association, *Heart Facts 1978*. New York: American Heart Association, Inc., 1977.

9. Andrew, George M., Becklake, Margaret R., Guleria, J. S. and Bates, C. V., Heart and lung functions in swimmers and nonathletes during growth. *Journal of Applied Physiology*, 32:245-251, 1972.

10. Barritt, D. W., Alimentary lipaemia in men with coronary artery disease and in controls. *British Medical Journal*, 2:640-644, 1956.

11. Becker, C. H., Meyer, Jacob and Necheles, H., Fat absorption and atherosclerosis. *Science*, 110:529-530, 1949.

12. Benson, N. Y. and Zauner, C. W., Physical working capacity of competitive swimmers following quantity and quality training and under contrasting ambient conditions. *Swimming Technique,* 13:13-15, 1976.

13. Bergstrom, Jonas, Hermansen, Lars, Hultman, Eric and Saltin, Bengt, Diet, muscle glycogen and physical performance, *Acta Physiologica Scandinavica,* 71:140-150, 1967.

14. Bjure, J., Pulmonary diffusing capacity for carbon monoxide in relation to cardiac output in man. *Scandinavian Journal of Clinical and Laboratory Investigation,* 17:1-113, 1965.

15. Black, Donald F, *The Relationship of Static Torque to Performance of Age-Group Swimmers,* unpublished thesis, University of Florida, 1973.

16. Blackburn, H., et al., Premature ventricular complexes induced by stress testing. *The American Journal of Cardiology,* 31:441-449, 1972.

17. Blackburn, H., et al., The electrocardiogram during exercise. *Circulation,* 34:1034-1043, 1968.

18. Bouchier, I. A. and Bronte-Stewart, B., Alimentary lipaemia and ischaemic heart-disease. *Lancet* 1:363-368, 1961.

19. Brunner, Caniel, Loebl, Kurt and Altman, Shmuel, Six-week nutritional trial with a reducing diet in a collective settlement: effect on serum lipids and body weight. *Circulation,* 30 (Supplement III):III-56, 1964.

20. Burke, E. J. and Hultgren, P. B., Will physicians of the future be able to prescribe exercise? *Journal of Medical Education,* 50:624-626, 1975.

21. Cade, J. Robert, Jogging in the heat. Paper presented as second in the series, *Fitness and Health,* North Florida Regional Hospital, June 23, 1978.

22. Carlson, Lars A., Serum lipids in normal men. *Acta Medica Scandinavica,* 167:377-397, 1960.

23. Carter, J. E. L. and Phillips, W. H., Structural changes in exercising middle-aged males during a 2-year period. *Journal of Applied Physiology,* 27:787-793, 1969.

24. Claremont, A. D., Taking winter in stride requires proper attire. *The Physician and Sportsmedicine,* 1:65-68, 1976.

25. Clarke, H. H., (ed.), Physical activity during menstruation and pregnancy. *Physical Fitness Research Digest,* 8:1-25, 1978.

26. Committee on Exercise and Physical Fitness, Evaluation for exercise prescription. *Journal of the American Medical Association,* 219:900-901, 1972.

27. Corbin, Charles B., Standards of subcutaneous fat applied to percentile norms for elementary school children. *American Journal of Clinical Nutrition,* 22:836-841, 1969.

28. Costill, D. L., Coyle, E., Dalsky, G., Evans, W., Fink, W. and Hoopes, D., Effects of elevated plasma FFA and insulin on muscle glycogen usage during exercise. *Journal of Applied Physiology: Respiratory Environmental and Exercise Physiology,* 43:695-699, 1977.

29. Costill, D. L., Dalsky, G. P. and Fink, W. J., Effects of caffeine ingestion on metabolism and exercise performance. *Medicine and Science in Sports,* 10:155-158, 1978.

30. Costill, David L., Sparks, Kenneth, Gregor, Robert and Turner, Craig, Muscle glycogen utilization during exhaustive running. *Journal of Applied Physiology,* 31:353-356, 1971.

31. Costill, David L. and Winrow, E., Maximal oxygen intake among marathon runners. *Archives of Physical Medicine and Rehabilitation,* 51:317-320, 1970.

32. Crews, Eugene L. III, Fuge, K. William, Oscai, Lawrence B., Holloszy, John O. and Shank, Robert E., Weight, food intake and body composition: effects of exercise and of protein deficiency. *American Journal of Physiology,* 216:359-363, 1969.

33. Cromwell, G. E., Report — Competitive athletics commitee on school health of the American academy of pediatrics. *Journal of School Health,* 27:173-175, 1957.

34. Cunningham, David A. and Eynon, Robert B., The working capacity of young competitive swimmers, 10-16 years of age. *Medicine and Science in Sports,* 5:227-231, 1973.

35. Cunningham, David A. and Hill, J. Stanley, Effect of training on cardiovascular response to exercise in women. *Journal of Applied Physiology,* 39:891-895, 1975.

36. Daniels, J. and Oldridge, N., Changes in oxygen consumption of young boys during growth and running training. *Medicine and Science in Sports,* 3:161-165, 1971.

37. Dehn, Michael M. and Bruce, Robert A., Longitudinal variations in maximal oxygen intake with age and activity. *Journal of Applied Physiology,* 33:805-807, 1972.

38. Dressendorfer, Rudolph H., Physical training during pregnancy and lactation. *The Physician and Sports-medicine,* 6:74, 75, 78, 80, 1978.

39. Drinkwater, B. L., et al., Heat tolerance of female distance runners. *Annals of the New York Academy of Sciences,* 301:777-792, 1977.

40. Erdelyi, G. J., Gynecological survey of female athletes. *Journal of Sports Medicine and Physical Fitness,* 2:174-179, 1962.

41. Ferguson, R. J., et al., Effect of physical training on treadmill capacity, collateral circulation and progression of coronary disease. *The American Journal of Cardiology,* 34:764-769, 1974.

42. Fineberg, S. K., The realities of obesity and fad diets. *Nutrition Today,* 7:23-26, 1972.

43. Flint, M. Marilyn, Drinkwater, Barbara L. and Horvath, Steven M., Effects of training on women's response to submaximal exercise. *Medicine and Science in Sports,* 6:89-94, 1974.

44. Gertler, M. M., Ischemic heart disease, heredity and body build as affected by exercise. *Canadian Medical Association Journal,* 96:728-732, 1967.

45. Gisolfi, Carl V. and Copping, John R., Thermal effects of prolonged treadmill exercise in the heat. *Medicine and Science in Sports,* 6:108-113, 1974.

46. Gollnick, P. D., Armstrong, R. B., Sembrowich, W. L., Shepherd, R. E. and Saltin, B., Glycogen depletion pattern in human skeletal muscle fibers after heavy exercise. *Journal of Applied Physiology,* 34:615-618, 1973.

47. Goode, R. C., Virgin, A., Romet, T. T., Crawford, D., Duffin, J., Pallandi, T. and Woch, Z., Effects of a short period of physical activity in adolescent boys and girls. *Canadian Journal of Applied Sport Sciences, 1:241-249, 1976.*

48. Grimby, Gunnar, Nilsson, Nils Johan and Saltin, Bengt, Cardiac output during submaximal and maximal exercise in active middle-aged athletes. *Journal of Applied Physiology*, 21:1150-1156, 1966.

49. Grimby, Gunnar and Saltin, Bengt, Physiological analysis of physically well-trained middle-aged and old athletes. *Acta Medica Scandinavica*, 179:513-526, 1966.

50. Gsell, Daniela and Mayer, Jean, Low blood cholesterol associated with high calorie, high saturated fat intakes in a Swiss alpine village population. *American Journal of Clinical Nutrition*, 10:471-479, 1962.

51. Guyton, A. C., *Textbook of Medical Physiology* (6th ed.). Philadelphia: W. B. Saunders Co., 1980.

52. Hale, C. H., Physiological maturity of little league baseball players. *Research Quarterly*, 28:276-284, 1956.

53. Hanson, John S. and Nedde, William H., Long-term physical training effect in sedentary females. *Journal of Applied Physiology*, 37:112-116, 1974.

54. Haralambie, G., Department of Performance and Sports Medicine, Medical University Clinic, Frieburg in Breisgau, West Germany, Personal Communication.

55. Harlan, William R., Jr., Oberman, Albert, Mitchell, Roert E. and Graybiel, Ashton, Constitutional and environmental factors related to serum lipid and lipoprotein levels. *Annals of Internal Medicine*, 66:540-555, 1967.

56. Hartung, G. H., Smolensky, M. H., Harris, R. B., Rangel, R. and Skrovan, C., Effects of varied durations of training on improvement in cardiorespiratory endurance. *Journal of Human Ergology*, 6:61-68, 1977.

57. Hashim, S. A., Felch, W. C. and Van Itallie, T. B., Lipid metabolism in relation to physiology and pathology of atherosclerosis. In: Hamilton, W. F. and Dow, P. (eds.), *Handbook of Physiology 2: Circulation II*. Washington, D.C.: American Physiological Society, 1963.

58. Hay, E., Considerations on women's sport. *Swimming Technique*, 15:38-39, 1978.

59. Hay, J. C., *The Biomechanics of Sports Techniques* (2nd ed.). Englewood Cliffs, N.J.: Prentice-Hall, Inc., 1978.

60. Hellerstein, H. K., Exercise tests inadequate for cardiac patients. *The Physician and Sportsmedicine*, 1:58-62, 1976.

61. Hellstrom, Richard, Serum lipids in male patients hospitalized for myocardial infarction. *Acta Medica Scandinavica*, 182:727-736, 1967.

62. Hermansen, Lars, Hultman, Eric and Saltin, Bengt, Muscle glycogen during prolonged severe exercise. *Acta Physiologica Scandinavica*, 71:129-139, 1967.

63. Hermansen, Lars and Osnes, Jan-Bjorn, Blood and muscle pH after maximal exercise in man. *Journal of Applied Physiology*, 32:304-308, 1972.

64. Hickson, R. C., Rennie, M. J., Conlee, R. K., Winder, W. W. and Holloszy, J. O., Effects of increased plasma fatty acids on glycogen utilization and endurance. *Journal of Applied Physiology: Respiratory, Environmental and Exercise Physiology*, 43:829-833, 1977.

65. Hilgard, Ernest R., *Hypnotic Susceptibility*. New York: Harcourt, Brace and World, Inc., 1956.

66. Holmgren, A. and Linderholm, H., Oxygen and carbon dioxide tensions of arterial blood during heavy and exhaustive exercise. *Acta Physiologica Scandinavica*, 44:203-215, 1958.

67. Holmgren, A., Mossfeldt, F., Sjostrand, T. and Strom, G., Effect of training on work capacity, total hemoglobin, blood volume, heart volume and pulse rate in recumbent and upright positions. *Acta Physiologica Scandinavica*, 50:72-83, 1960.

68. Holloszy, John O., Skinner, James S., Toro, Gelson and Cureton, Thomas K., Effects of a six-month program of endurance exercise on the serum lipids of middle-aged men. *American Journal of Cardiology*, 14:753-760, 1964.

69. Holyoak, O. J., Allen, R. E., Pennypacker, H. S. Jr., Hall, D. and Zauner, C. W., A profile of the psychological characteristics of age-group swimmers. *Proceedings, 79th Annual Meeting, NCPEAM*, 125-140, 1976.

70. Hoxie, J., Competitive athletics for children. *American Medical Association Journal*, 168:1439-1440, 1958.

71. Issekutz, Bela, Jr., Issekutz, Andrew C. and Nash, Dennis, Mobilization of energy sources in exercising dogs. *Journal of Applied Physiology*, 29:691-697, 1970.

72. Jette, M., Thoden, J. S. and Gauthier, R., Aerobic exer-

cise prescription intensity in terms of maximal working capacity. *Canadian Journal of Public Health,* 66:465-467, 1975.

73. Johnson, P. B., Updyke, W. F., Stolberg, D. C. and Schaefer, M., *Physical Education: A Problem Solving Approach to Health and Fitness.* New York: Holt, Rinehart and Winston, 1966.

74. Joint Committee on Athletics for Children of Elementary and Junior High School Age, Desirable athletics for children. *American Association for Health, Physical Education and Recreation,* 23:21-22, 1952.

75. Jokl, Ernst and Jokl, Peter, *The Physiological Basis of Athletic Records.* Springfield, Ill.: Charles C. Thomas, 1968.

76. Jones, N. L., Campbell, E. J., Edwards, R. H. T. and Robertson, D. G., *Clinical Exercise Testing.* Philadelphia: W. B. Saunders Co., 1975.

77. Jobsis, F. F. and Stainsby, W. N., Oxidation of NADH during contraction of circulated mamalian skeletal muscle. *Respiration Physiology,* 4:292-300, 1968.

78. Karlsson, Jan and Saltin, Bengt, Diet, muscle glycogen and endurance performance. *Journal of Applied Physiology,* 31:203-206, 1971.

79. Kasch, F. W., Phillips, W. H., Carter, J. E. L. and Boyer, J. L., Cardiovascular changes in middle-aged men during two years of training. *Journal of Applied Physiology,* 34:53-57, 1973.

80. Kattus, A. A., Exercise testing and therapy in ischemic heart disease. *Journal of the South Carolina Medical Association,* 65, Supplement: 57-60, 1969.

81. Katz, L. N. and Pick, R., The role of endocrines, stress and heredity on atherosclerosis. In: Hamilton, W. F. and Dow, P. (eds.), *Handbook of Physiology 2: Circulation II.* Washington, D.C.: American Physiological Society, 1963.

82. Kavanaugh, T., Postcoronary joggers need precise guidelines. *The Physician and Sportsmedicine,* 1:63-66, 1976.

83. Kavanaugh, T., Shephard, R. J., Doney, H. and Pandit, V., Intensive exercise in coronary rehabilitation. *Medicine and Science in Sports,* 5:34-39, 1973.

84. Keul, J., Haralambie, G., Bruder, M. and Gottstein, H.-J., The effect of weight lifting exercise on heart rate and metabolism in experienced weight lifters. *Medicine and Science in Sports,* 10:13-15, 1978.

85. Keys, Ancel, et al., Epidemiological studies related to coronary heart disease: characteristics of men aged 40-59 in seven countries. *Acta Medica Scandinavica,* Supplement 460:1-392, 1966.

86. Kilbom, Asa, Physical training in women. *The Scandinavian Journal of Clinical and Laboratory Investigation,* 28, Supplementum 119:1-34, 1971.

87. Kilbom, Asa and Astrand, Irma, Physical training with submaximal intensities in women. *Scandinavian Journal of Clinical and Laboratory Investigation,* 28:163-165, 171.

88. Kraus, H., Raab, W. and White, P. D., *Hypokinetic Disease.* Springfield, Ill.: Charles C. Thomas, Publisher, 1961.

89. Krogman, W. M., Child growth and football. *Journal of Health, Physical Education and Recreation,* 26:12, 1955.

90. Lamb, David R., *Physiology of Exercise.* New York: Macmillan Publishing Co., Inc., 1978.

91. LeCron, Leslie M., *Self Hypnotism.* New York: The New American Library, Inc., 1970.

92. MacAlpin, R. N. and Kattus, A. A., Adaptation to exercise in angina pectoris: the electrocardiogram during treadmill walking and coronary angiographic findings. *Circulation,* 33:183-201, 1966.

93. MacDougal, J. Duncan, et al., Effects of metabolic hyperthermia on performance during heavy prolonged exercise. *Journal of Applied Physiology,* 36:538-544, 1974.

94. Magel, John R. and Anderson, K. L., Pulmonary diffusing capacity and cardiac output in young trained Norwegian swimmers and untrained subjects. *Medicine and Science in Sports,* 1:131-139, 1969.

95. Maksim, G, Desirable athletics for children. *American Medical Association Journal,* 168:1431-1433, 1958.

96. Mathews, D. K. and Fox, E. L., *The Physiological Basis of Physical Education and Athletics.* Philadelphia: W. B. Saunders, Co., 1976.

97. McCrimmon, D. R., et al., Effect of training on plasma catecholamines in post myocardial infarction patients. *Medicine and Science in Sports*, 8:152-156, 1976.

98. Mellerowicz, Herold, The effect of training on heart and circulation and its importance in preventive cardiology. In: Raab, Wilhelm (ed.), *Prevention of Ischemic Heart Disease: Principles and Practice*. Springfield, Ill.: Charles C. Thomas, 1966.

99. Merriman, J. E., The overweight physician. *Cardiac Rehabilitation*, 5:5-8, 1974.

100. Montoye, H. J., et al., Habitual physical activity and serum lipids: males, age 16-64 in a total community. *Journal of Chronic Disease*, 29:697-709, 1976.

101. Morehouse, Laurence E. and Miller, Augustus T., Jr., *Physiology of Exercise* (7th ed.). St. Louis: The C.V. Mosby Co., 1976.

102. O'Hara, W. J., Allen, C. and Shephard, R. J., Treatment of obesity by exercise in the cold. *Canadian Medical Association Journal*, 117:773-778, 1977.

103. Osnes, Jan-Bjorn and Hermansen, Lars, Acid-base balance after maximal exercise of short duration. *Journal of Applied Physiology*, 32:59-63, 1972.

104. Pernow, Bengt and Saltin, Bengt, Availability of substrates and capacity for prolonged heavy exercise in man. *Journal of Applied Physiology*, 31:416-422, 1971.

105. Pollock, Michael L., How much exercise is enough? *The Physician and Sportsmedicine*, 6:1-11, 1978.

106. Pollock, Michael L., Physiological characteristics of older champion track athletes. *Research Quarterly*, 45:363-373, 1974.

107. Pollock, M. L., et al., Physiologic responses of men 49 to 65 years of age to endurance training. *Journal of the American Geriatrics Society*, 24:97-104, 1976.

108. Pollock, Michael L., et al., Effects of mode of training on cardiovascular function and body composition of adult men. *Medicine and Science in Sports*, 7:139-145, 1975.

109. Pollock, Michael L., et al., Effects of walking on body composition and cardiovascular function of middle-aged men. *Journal of Applied Physiology*, 30:126-130, 1971.

110. Pollock, Michael L., Miller, Herny S., Jr. and Wilmore,

Jack, A profile of a champion distance runner: age 60. *Medicine and Science in Sports*, 6:118-121, 1974.

111. Pollock, Michael L., Miller, Henry S., Jr. and Wilmore, Jack, Physiological characteristics of champion American track athletes 40 to 75 years of age. *Journal of Gerontology*, 29:645-649, 1974.

112. Pollock, M. L., Ward, A. and Ayres, J. J., Cardiorespiratory fitness: response to differing intensities and durations of training. *Archives of Physical Medicine and Rehabilitation*, *58:467-473, 1977.*

113. *Rechnitzer, P. A., et al., A controlled prospective study of the effect of endurance training on the recurrence rate of myocardial infarction. American Journal of Epidemiology,* 102:358-365, 1975.

114. Regan, T. J., et al., Myocardial blood flow and oxygen consumption during postprandial lipemia and heparin induced lipolysis. *Circulation,* 23:55-63, 1961.

115. Reichert, J. L., Competitive athletics for pre-teen-age children. *American Medical Association Journal,* 166:1701-1707, 1958.

116. Rosenblatt, Gerald, Stokes, Joseph, III and Bassett, David R., Whole blood viscosity, hematocrit and serum lipid levels in normal subjects and patients with coronary heart disease. *Journal of Laboratory and Clinical Medicine,* 65:202-211, 1965.

117. Ryan, A. J., *Medical Care of the Athlete.* New York: The McGraw Hill Book Co., Inc., 1962.

118. Saltin, B. and Grimby, G., Physiological analysis of middle-aged and old former athletes: comparison with still active athletes of the same ages. *Circulation,* 38:1104-1115, 1968.

119. Selye, Hans, *The Physiology and Pathology of Exposure to Stress.* Montreal: Acta, Inc., 1950.

120. Shane, Stanley R., Relation between serum lipids and physical conditioning. *American Journal of Cardiology,* 18:540-543, 1966.

121. Sheldon, W. H., *The Varieties of Human Physique.* New York: Harper and Brothers Publishers, 1940.

122. Shephard, Roy J., *Endurance Fitness.* Toronto: University of Toronto Press, 1969.

123. Sidney, K. H. and Shephard, Roy J., Frequency and intensity of exercise training for elderly subjects. *Medicine and Science in Sports,* 10:125-131, 1978.

124. Soto, K. I. and Zauner, C. W., Cardiac output in trained preadolescent competitive swimmers and in untrained normal children. *The Physiologist,* 20:89, 1977.

125. Stumpe, Jill, Physiological Response to Exercise in College-Age Females During Prolonged Use of an Oral Contraceptive, unpublished thesis, University of Florida, 1976.

126. Sundstrom, Gunnar, Zauner, Christian W. and Arborelius, Mans, Jr., Decrease in pulmonary diffusing capacity during lipid infusion in healthy men. *Journal of Applied Physiology,* 34:816-820, 1973.

127. Sutton, John R., Hormonal and metabolic responses to exercise in subjects of high and low work capacities. *Medicine and Science in Sports,* 10:1-6, 1978.

128. Swenson, Edward W. and Zauner, Christian W., Effects of physical conditioning on pulmonary function and working capacity in middle-aged men. *Scandinavian Journal of Respiratory Disease,* 48:378-383, 1967.

129. Taylor, A. W., Lappage, R. and Ras, S., Skeletal muscle glycogen stores after submaximal and maximal work. *Medicine and Science in Sports,* 3:75-78, 1971.

130. Ullyot, Joan, *Women's Running.* Mountain View, California: World Publications, 1976.

131. Vaccaro, P., Zauner, C. W. and Updyke, W. F., Resting and exercise respiratory function in well-trained child swimmers. *Journal of Sports Medicine and Physical Fitness,* 17:297-306, 1977.

132. Wells, C. L., et al., Physical working capacity and maximal oxygen uptake of teenaged athletes. *Medicine and Science in Sports,* 5:232-238, 1973.

133. Wilmore, J. H., Exercise prescription: role of the physiatrist and allied health professional. *Archives of Physical Medicine and Rehabilitation,* 57:315-319, 1976.

134. Wilmore, J. H., Brown, C. H. and Davis, J. A., Body physique and composition of the female distance runner. *Annals of the New York Academy of Sciences,* 301:764-776, 1977.

135. Wilmore, J. H., Miller, H. L., Jr. and Pollock, M. L., Body composition and physiological characteristics of active endurance athletes in their eighth decade of life. *Medicine and Science in Sports,* 6:44-48, 1974.

136. Wilmore, Jack H., et al., Physiological alterations resulting from a 10-week program of jogging. *Medicine and Science in Sports,* 2:7-14, 1970.

137. Yost, L. J., Zauner, C. W. and Jaeger, M. J., Pulmonary diffusing capacity and physical working capacity in young competitive swimmers and untrained youths. *Respiration,* in press (1981).

138. Zauner, C. W., The relationship of age and habitual activity level to fasting and postprandial lipemia. *Journal of Sports Medicine and Physical Fitness,* 8:201-211, 1968.

139. Zauner, C. W. and Benson, N. Y., Effect of physical training upon postprandial lipemia in men with abnormal responses to the oral fat tolerance test. *Journal of Sports Medicine and Physical Fitness,* 17:381-386, 1977.

140. Zauner, C. W. and Benson, N. Y., Physiological alterations observed in young competitive swimmers during three years of intensive training. *Medicine and Science in Sports,* 9:53, 1977.

141. Zauner, Christian W., Burt, John J. and Mapes, Donald F., The effect of strenuous and mild pre-meal exercise on postprandial lipemia. *Research Quarterly,* 39:395-401, 1968.

142. Zauner, C. W., Fencl, J. and Swenson, E. W., Physiological characteristics of young, well-trained female swimmers and runners. *Medicine and Science in Sports,* 6:87, 1974.

143. Zauner, C. W., Kaufmann, D. A. and Benson, N. Y., Effect of protein dietary supplement on body composition of swimmers. *Swimming Technique,* 13:120-122, 1977.

144. Zauner, C. W. and Reese, E. C., Specific training, taper and fatigue. *Track Technique, 49:1546-1550, 1972.*

145. Astrand, P.-O. and Rodahl, K., *Textbook of Work Physiology* (2nd ed.). New York: McGraw-Hill Book Co., 1977.

Notes

Norma Y. Benson received her bachelor's degree from the University of Arkansas at Monticello and her master's from the University of Florida. She taught for 13 years in the Palatka, Florida, public school system, serving as department chairman for girls physical education, Palatka South High School, 1968-1970. During the academic year 1974-1975, Ms. Benson served as a Florida Lung Association Fellow in the Center for Physical and Motor Fitness, University of Florida, at which time she participated in studies of physiological characteristics of child and female athletes. Her work has been reported in such scientific journals as *Medicine and Science in Sports, Journal of Sports Medicine and Physical Fitness, Swimming Technique* and *Journal of the Florida Medical Association.* A frequent lecturer to various community organizations, Ms. Benson has also presented research findings at scientific sessions of the Florida Association for Health, Physical Education and Recreation and of the American College of Sports Medicine.

Presently employed as Director, Adult Fitness, Putnam Community Hospital, Norma Benson and husband Craig continue residence in Palatka. They have two children, Shelley and Kim. The Bensons are avid joggers and road racers.

About the Authors

Christian W. Zauner holds the bachelor's degree from West Chester (Pennsylvania) State College, the master's from Syracuse University and the Ph.D. from Southern Illinois University. He has done postdoctoral work at Malmö General Hospital, Malmö, Sweden. Following two years at Temple University as an assistant professor he came to the University of Florida where he is presently professor of Professional Physical Education and Medicine. He is a Fellow of the American College of Sports Medicine and has similar status with the American-Scandinavian Foundation. Research interests include the child athlete, blood lipid metabolism, physiological outcomes of endurance training and the relationship between habitual physical activity and aging. Dr. Zauner has published more than 50 scientific reports in such journals as *Respiration, Journal of Applied Physiology, Medicine and Science in Sports, Scandinavian Journal of Respiratory Diseases,* and *Journal of Sports Medicine and Physical Fitness.* He is a frequent lecturer and has spoken to numerous scientific and professional groups including The American College of Sports Medicine and The American Physiological Society.

Dr. Zauner resides in Gainesville, Florida with his wife, Betty, and with his three children. He has been jogging for more than 20 years with frequent involvement in road racing and in biathalon competition.